W9-BOP-844

DISCARD

Censorship
in Ray Bradbury's
Fahrenheit 451

Other Books in the Social Issues in Literature Series:

Social Issues
in Literature

Censorship
in Ray Bradbury's
Fahrenheit 451

Candice L. Mancini, Book Editor

GREENHAVEN PRESS
A part of Gale, Cengage Learning

Detroit • New York • San Francisco • New Haven, Conn • Waterville, Maine • London

GALE
CENGAGE Learning™

Christine Nasso, *Publisher*
Elizabeth Des Chenes, *Managing Editor*

© 2011 Greenhaven Press, a part of Gale, Cengage Learning

Gale and Greenhaven Press are registered trademarks used herein under license.

For more information, contact:
Greenhaven Press
27500 Drake Rd.
Farmington Hills, MI 48331-3535
Or you can visit our Internet site at gale.cengage.com

ALL RIGHTS RESERVED.
No part of this work covered by the copyright herein may be reproduced, transmitted, stored, or used in any form or by any means graphic, electronic, or mechanical, including but not limited to photocopying, recording, scanning, digitizing, taping, Web distribution, information networks, or information storage and retrieval systems, except as permitted under Section 107 or 108 of the 1976 United States Copyright Act, without the prior written permission of the publisher.

For product information and technology assistance, contact us at

Gale Customer Support, 1-800-877-4253
For permission to use material from this text or product, submit all requests online at www.cengage.com/permissions

Further permissions questions can be emailed to permissionrequest@cengage.com

Articles in Greenhaven Press anthologies are often edited for length to meet page requirements. In addition, original titles of these works are changed to clearly present the main thesis and to explicitly indicate the author's opinion. Every effort is made to ensure that Greenhaven Press accurately reflects the original intent of the authors. Every effort has been made to trace the owners of copyrighted material.

Cover photograph copyright © Bettmann/Corbis.

LIBRARY OF CONGRESS CATALOGING-IN-PUBLICATION DATA

Censorship in Ray Bradbury's Fahrenheit 451 / Candice L. Mancini, Book Editor.
p. cm. -- (Social issues in literature)
Includes bibliographical references and index.
ISBN 978-0-7377-5288-5 (hardcover) -- ISBN 978-0-7377-5289-2 (pbk.)
1. Bradbury, Ray, 1920- Fahrenheit 451. 2. Book burning in literature. 3. Censorship in literature. I. Mancini, Candice.
PS3503.R167F334 2011
813'.54--dc22

2010043632

Printed in the United States of America
2 3 4 5 6 7 15 14 13 12 11

Contents

In *Fahrenheit 451*, Ray Bradbury reminds readers that even if you can kill a book, you cannot kill its ideas.

Chapter 3: Contemporary Perspectives on Censorship

Introduction

Communities are wary whenever school boards, school administrators, and legislators use the argument of social inappropriateness to rationalize censoring what students read or write. There is no collective definition of social inappropriateness among any society; further, among differing cultures and historical times, what is deemed socially unacceptable behavior varies greatly. Any society that hopes to encourage diversity and respect for others does itself a disservice when it carelessly tosses around blanket condemnations. As philosopher John Stuart Mill stated in *On Liberty* (1859), "We can never be sure that the opinion we are endeavoring to stifle is a false opinion; and if we were sure, stifling it would be an evil still."

Even if one could argue against Mill, the information society that permeates much of the globe today makes unrealistic the plausibility of reining in knowledge seeking. Although the World Wide Web allows for infinite knowledge seeking, too many Internet sources—in addition to being deemed socially inappropriate—are unsubstantiated and of limited credibility. But banning books and limiting other sources on the basis of social inappropriateness diminishes students' ability to distinguish between sources that are and are not credible. Former president of Yale University Alfred Whitney Griswold stated the quandary well in a February 24, 1959, *New York Times* article: "Books won't stay banned. They won't burn. Ideas won't go to jail. In the long run of history, the censor and the inquisitor have always lost. The only weapon against bad ideas is better ideas."

It is through the First Amendment to the US Constitution that citizens are afforded the right to freedom of expression. Because of the First Amendment, a parent is well within his or her rights to express, in writing or out loud, for example: "I do not like this book my teenager is reading because it depicts homosexuality and I do not agree with homosexuality." But if that parent cherishes the right to speak such sentiments, he or she must acknowledge that another parent has the right to deem the same book worthy because it represents homosexuality as a normal part of society.

Ray Bradbury's novel *Fahrenheit 451* is an important reminder of the dangers of stifling the First Amendment. First, it depicts the horrors of living in a police state, including the punishments people endure for breaking the rules: detractors are imprisoned, disappear, are hunted down, or have their homes burned to the ground. The most haunting dangers, however, may be the least obvious. Those who do stay within the confines of some collective definition of social appropriateness suffer a far worse fate, as the character Mildred Montag illustrates. She is brainwashed by television, attempts suicide, is addicted to pills, and is devoid of empathy and understanding. Mildred's apathy—to society, to knowledge, to relationships, and to life itself—represents the grim product of a humanity denied free access to information.

The articles that follow explore censorship as portrayed by Bradbury in *Fahrenheit 451* and examine the ongoing issue of censorship today.

Chronology

1920
Ray Bradbury is born on August 22 in Waukegan, Illinois, to Leo Bradbury and Esther Moberg Bradbury.

1945
Bradbury takes a two-month-long road trip to Mexico with a friend, which influences many of his later stories, including "The Highway" (1950), "En La Noche" (1952), and "Sun and Shadow" (1953).

1947
Bradbury marries Marguerite (Maggie) McClure, whom he would later credit as a major influence on his writing career. Bradbury's first book, *Dark Carnival*, is published.

1949
The couple's first daughter, Susan, is born. Three more daughters will follow: Ramona, Bettina, and Alexandra.

1950
Bradbury publishes *The Martian Chronicles*, a collection of science fiction stories that criticize, among other things, imperialism, censorship, and the nuclear arms race.

1952
The Bradbury Review, a fanzine, is created, establishing Bradbury's solid footing as a distinguished science-fiction writer.

1953
Bradbury publishes *Fahrenheit 451*, which he draws from his short story "Bright Phoenix" and which is blatantly critical of censorship and too much government control. Bradbury travels to Ireland to write the screenplay for John Huston's film version of *Moby Dick*.

1957

Bradbury publishes *Dandelion Wine*, a highly autobiographical young-adult novel based on his memories of growing up in Waukegan, Illinois.

1962

Bradbury publishes *Something Wicked This Way Comes.*

1964

Bradbury serves as creative consultant on the United States Pavilion at the 1964 New York World's Fair.

1977

Bradbury is given the World Fantasy Award for Lifetime Achievement.

1985

Bradbury receives the PEN Literary Award for his body of work.

1993

Bradbury receives an Emmy Award for his animated holiday special *The Halloween Tree*, which is based on his 1972 novel of the same name.

1999

Bradbury suffers a near-fatal stroke. While in the hospital, he continues to write.

2000

Bradbury is awarded the National Book Foundation's Medal for Distinguished Contribution to American Letters.

2002

Bradbury receives a star on the Hollywood Walk of Fame.

2003

Maggie Bradbury dies.

2004

Bradbury is given the National Medal of Arts, the highest honor awarded to artists and art patrons by the US government.

2005

Sam Weller's authorized biography of Bradbury, *The Bradbury Chronicles*, is published.

2010

Los Angeles declares August 22–28 Ray Bradbury Week in honor of his ninetieth birthday.

Social Issues
in Literature

CHAPTER 1

| Background on
Ray Bradbury

The Life of Ray Bradbury

Gary K. Wolfe

Gary K. Wolfe, professor of humanities and English at Roosevelt University's Evelyn T. Stone College of Professional Studies, is a scholar and critic of science fiction, fantasy, and horror.

In the following viewpoint, Wolfe examines Ray Bradbury's childhood, pointing out how the author's early years influenced his writing later in life. Such a focus on the past instead of the future makes Bradbury an anomaly in the science-fiction world. Also, although he is widely regarded for his science-fiction work, Bradbury's range includes many styles and often focuses on contemporary social issues such as immigration, alienation, and racism.

Although Ray Bradbury remains perhaps the best known of all science-fiction writers, and although his stories and themes have permeated all areas of American culture as have those of no other science-fiction writer—through more than five hundred stories, poems, essays, plays, films, television plays, radio, music, and even comic books—Bradbury is still something of an anomaly in the genre. In a field that thrives on the fantastic and the marvelous, Bradbury's best stories celebrate the mundane; in a field preoccupied with the future, Bradbury's vision is firmly rooted in the past—both his own personal past and the past of America. In a popular genre where reputations, until recently, have been made through ingenious plotting and the exposition of scientific and technological ideas, Bradbury built an enormous reputation virtually on style alone—and then, when the rest of the writers in the

Gary K. Wolfe, "Ray (Douglas) Bradbury," in *Twentieth-Century American Science-Fiction Writers*, ed. David Cowart and Thomas L. Wymer. *Dictionary of Literary Biography, vol. 8*, part 1. Copyright © 1981 Gale, a part of Cengage Learning, Inc. Reproduced by permission.

genre began to discover the uses of stylistic experimentation, turned ever more toward self-imitation and the recapitulation of earlier themes. When science fiction seemed almost exclusively a literature of technophiles, Bradbury became a lone symbol of the dangers of technology, even to the point of refusing to drive an automobile or fly in an airplane. But when science fiction came increasingly to adopt an ambivalent attitude toward unchecked technological progress, Bradbury became an international spokesman for the virtues of spaceflight and technological achievement. Clearly Bradbury cannot be accused of following the dominant trends in science fiction or even of literature in general. He is his own most important referent, and despite his widely avowed love of earlier writers from Edgar Allan Poe to Thomas Wolfe to Ernest Hemingway, it is in Bradbury's own Midwestern background that one finds the most important sources for his fiction.

Bradbury's Childhood Shaped His Writing

Bradbury is perhaps the most autobiographical of science-fiction writers, and this, too, seems anomalous: how, after all, can one construct meaningful future worlds from so much reference to the past and so little to the present? One answer, of course, is that Bradbury's science fiction is, in fact, seldom extrapolative [using historical data to make inferences about the future], for the values Bradbury seeks to express are the values he associates with his own past. Bradbury was born on 22 August 1920 and spent most of his childhood in Waukegan, Illinois, a small community on the western shore of Lake Michigan, which was to become the "Green Town" of many later stories. Early in life he was introduced to the world of fantasy and the supernatural. By the time he was six, he had seen several horror movies—notably *The Cat and the Canary*, and Lon Chaney's *The Hunchback of Notre Dame* and *The Phantom of the Opera*—and had developed a morbid fear of the dark. (His 1955 children's book, *Switch on the Night*, was based on these memories and designed to allay the fear of darkness for his own children.) His Aunt Neva, whose name was given to a character in a few stories and who received the dedication of the 1953 collection *The Golden Apples of the Sun*, introduced him to fairy tales and to the Oz books of L. Frank Baum, whom Bradbury later counted among his chief influences. Bradbury's father, Leonard Spaulding Bradbury, worked as a lineman for the Waukegan Bureau of Power and Light. Not only did "Leonard Spaulding" later become a Bradbury pseudonym, but even his father's mundane occupation was transformed into romance in the 1948 story "Powerhouse," collected in *The Golden Apples of the Sun*. . . .

Twice during his childhood, in 1926–1927 and again in 1932–1933, Bradbury lived with his family in Arizona, where his father hoped to find work after being laid off during the Depression. It is possible that these early impressions of the desert affected his later visions of Mars, and perhaps his sensitive views of Mexican-Americans as well. But both moves were abortive, and in both cases the family returned to Waukegan. The Bradburys did not move west permanently until their 1934 move to Los Angeles. Bradbury dates his career choice from about this time: at the age of fifteen, he began submitting short stories to major national magazines, hoping ultimately for a sale to the *Saturday Evening Post* but receiving no acceptance. Encouraged by sympathetic high school literature teachers, however, he became active in his school's drama classes and wrote for school publications.

Early Writing Opportunities

In 1937 Bradbury's first real connection with the world of science fiction began when he joined the Los Angeles Science Fiction League. Here he met Henry Kuttner, a budding professional writer whose first story was published that same year and who would become something of a mentor to the younger writer. The league's fanzine, *Imagination!*, printed Bradbury's

Novelist Ray Bradbury, who addresses censorship in his novel Fahrenheit 451. Jon Kopaloff/Getty Images.

first published short story, "Hollerbochen's Dilemma," in 1938, and his increasing involvement as a science-fiction fan led him, in 1939, to begin his own mimeographed publication, *Futuria Fantasia*. That same year he attended the World Science Fiction convention in New York and visited the New York World's Fair.

At the age of twenty Bradbury was still living with his family and selling newspapers for income, but by this time a career as a writer seemed a real possibility. Bradbury had been listed in a national directory of fans of science fiction, and his letters were becoming familiar features of the letter columns of the professional pulp magazines. *Futuria Fantasia* lasted for only four issues, but in the last issue in 1940, Bradbury published a story called "The Piper," which gave early evidence of the central themes of *The Martian Chronicles* (1950). Aided by such professional writers as Robert Heinlein, Leigh Brackett, Jack Williamson, Edmond Hamilton, Ross Rocklynne, and Henry Hasse, he was finally able to break into professional markets in 1941 with "Pendulum," a story written in collaboration with Hasse that appeared in the November *Super Science Stories*. The following year he began selling stories to *Weird Tales*, which, though not a science-fiction pulp in the strictest sense, would prove during the next few years to be the most natural home for the fantasy and horror stories that would go to make up Bradbury's first collection, *Dark Carnival*. Bradbury soon discovered that his distinctive poetic style would be more readily welcomed by *Weird Tales*, a few detective magazines, and eventually the "slicks" such as *American Mercury*, *Charm*, and *Mademoiselle*, than by the science-fiction magazines he had so avidly read as a teenager.

By 1944 Bradbury, exempt from the draft because of his poor vision, seemed aware that style was his strong point and became more conscious of developing it. As a teenager he had been briefly infatuated with Thomas Wolfe; now he began to read writers whose work was more spare, more controlled, such as Jessamyn West, Sherwood Anderson, Eudora Welty, and Katherine Anne Porter. He was at the same time discovering new sources of material for his fiction. While selling newspapers in 1940, Bradbury had kept an office in a tenement inhabited largely by Mexican-Americans (whom he would feature prominently in several later stories). In 1945 his interest in Mexican culture deepened during a two-month-long automobile trip to Mexico when Bradbury accompanied an artist friend to collect masks for the Los Angeles County Museum. Bradbury was increasingly impressed with the growing sense of an alien culture whose values were different from those of the United States. . . .

What most impressed Bradbury about this trip to Mexico was the preoccupation with death that seemed to permeate much of the culture. The trip eventually led to Guanajuato, northwest of Mexico City, where Bradbury was horrified and fascinated by the underground catacombs with their upright rows of mummified remains. . . .

Bradbury's Early Wide Range

Bradbury's reputation as a short-story writer had by the mid 1940s reached the point where book publication began to seem a logical next step. August Derleth, the Wisconsin author who had established the small fantasy press Arkham House primarily to publish in book form the fiction of H.P. Lovecraft and his circle, accepted [Bradbury's] "The Lake" for his 1945 anthology *Who Knocks?* and suggested that Bradbury might prepare a whole volume of fantasy and horror stories for Arkham House. Don Congdon, a New York editor and agent who in 1947 became Bradbury's agent, also began to explore the idea of a collection. His career clearly on the upswing, Bradbury was so confident of his own future output that on the eve of his wedding to Marguerite McClure in 1947, he claims, he burned more than a million words of his earlier writing that he felt did not meet his current standards.

Bradbury's career also seemed to be moving rapidly in several directions at once. His first book, *Dark Carnival*, published by Arkham House in 1947, would bolster his reputation as a writer of weird fiction, but that was a kind of fiction that Bradbury was coming to write less and less frequently. From *Weird Tales* he had moved increasingly into such markets as *American Mercury, Mademoiselle, Charm, Harper's*, and the *New Yorker*, and his fiction was beginning to appear with some regularity in such mainstream collections as *The Best American Short Stories* and *Prize Stories: O. Henry Awards*. Even though many of his stories were fantasy and science fiction, Bradbury was gaining a reputation as a sensitive stylist who tackled the contemporary social issues of racism and illegal immigration of Mexicans into this country. . . .

One of Bradbury's most consistent themes in this early fiction was that of alienation—from technology, from a culture, even from the body itself. . . .

Bradbury Finds Success

Published in May 1950, *The Martian Chronicles* was a seminal event in the history of science fiction's growing respectability. The book was widely reviewed by a critical community that extended well beyond the science-fiction subculture, most notably by Christopher Isherwood, who praised it lavishly in the journal *Tomorrow*. Impressed by Bradbury's poetic language and unconcerned by his lack of even a semblance of scientific verisimilitude, many readers found in the book a profound exploration of the state of America in 1950 with its fears of nuclear war, its problems with racism and growing book censorship, its confused values, and its yearning for a simpler life. By November 1952 the book had gone through six printings and had appeared in England as *The Silver Locusts*; during the next several years it would remain constantly in print in paperback and be translated into more than thirty foreign-language editions, one of which (1955) featured an introduction by [Argentine novelist] Jorge Luis Borges.

Science-fiction readers have criticized *The Martian Chronicles* on the grounds that the Martian colonies of the book are little more than transplanted small towns from the American Midwest of the 1920s. But Bradbury was certainly conscious of this and has repeatedly maintained that his Mars is not a projection of the future but rather a mirror of American life. Indeed the subject matter of the book is more history than science, and what technology the book features is largely technology in the service of exploring new frontiers. Bradbury does not dwell on making his machines believable any more than he dwells on making his Mars astronomically accurate; his real concern, it may be argued, is to explore some of the key issues in American history—capitalism, technology, the family, the role of imagination—in a context free of historical constraints. . . .

By 1952 Bradbury's reputation was firmly established, and *The Ray Bradbury Review*, a fanzine, was devoted exclusively to his work. Bradbury began his involvement with Hollywood by providing an original screen story for a film that would eventually be released as *It Came from Outer Space* (1953). For Bantam Books he edited an anthology of fantasy fiction, *Timeless Stories for Today and Tomorrow* (1952), that clearly revealed his predilection for psychological symbolism over scientific extrapolation as a basis for fantastic fiction. His early horror fiction began to reappear in comic books. In August 1953 film director John Huston invited him to Ireland to work on the screenplay for *Moby Dick* (1956), and Bradbury's experiences with the Irish later proved a rich mine of material for stories and plays, just as his experiences with Mexicans had been eight years earlier. . . .

Fahrenheit 451

Later in 1953 Bradbury published what would become his only work to approach *The Martian Chronicles* in popularity and influence. *Fahrenheit 451* had been germinating as early as 1947 when Bradbury wrote a short story, "Bright Phoenix," about a small town whose residents foil government book burnings by each memorizing one of the censored texts. (Bradbury eventually published this story, in a slightly revised form, in the May 1963 issue of the *Magazine of Fantasy and Science Fiction*.) In 1951 this basic premise involving government book burners was expanded to novella length as *The Fireman*, which appeared in the February issue of *Galaxy*. Expanded again to twice the length of *The Fireman*, *Fahrenheit 451* became Bradbury's first and best novel.

Although hindsight invites the reader to view *Fahrenheit 451* as a passionate attack on censorship and perhaps on the McCarthyism of the early 1950s as well, the book is equally an attack on the growing power of a mass culture, particularly television, whose dynamics disallow complexity of thought and which consistently falls prey to the demands of special interest groups. Above all, the book-burning firemen of the novel are concerned that culture be made inoffensive, unthreatening, and universally accessible. Books, they feel, confuse citizens with contradictory values and ambivalent portrayals of human behavior. Beatty, the fireman supervisor who explains this to the protagonist Montag (who has begun to exhibit an unhealthy interest in the books he is burning), traces this tradition of book burning throughout American history; Benjamin Franklin, according to the history of the firemen, became America's first "fireman" in this new sense when he sought to limit the distribution of Royalist pamphlets in the colonies. The history is not as distorted as it may seem: one of the strengths of Bradbury's argument in the novel is that he sees book burning as not simply a totalitarian phenomenon, but one that has at least some roots in the process of democratization that led to the rise of American mass culture in the first place.

As with his other science-fiction settings, Bradbury makes little effort to paint a convincing portrait of a possible future society; instead, he strips the story of all but essential details, characters, and images that are needed to make his point. The novel takes place in what appears to be a totalitarian state, but the only real feature of this totalitarianism that the reader sees is the book burning, and even that does not seem to be in the service of any particular political philosophy. In fact, it is suggested that the totalitarianism of this state is simply mass culture enforced by law. Nor is there much evidence of technological advance in this future society: the chief image of technology is the Mechanical Hound, a rather baroque robot version of the traditional firemen's mascot, which is programmed to detect anomalous variations in body chemistry—presumably this is a hint of possible antisocial behavior—and to track down criminals like a real hound. Why a society given to the abolition of imagination would choose to cast its technology in such a bizarrely imaginative form as this is not explained, but as an image of the replacement by an ominous piece of machinery of a tradition of middle-class society the Hound is effective.

The novel ends when Montag, who has finally come to reject his role as a book burner and has murdered his supervisor Beatty, escapes a massive manhunt and joins a rural community of individuals who seek to preserve books by memorizing them. Whereas the society from which Montag has escaped is associated with the image of the salamander—the destructive fire-lizard—his new society associates itself instead with the image of the phoenix, rising from the ashes of the burning books. Culture, Bradbury says, periodically undergoes such self-destructive convulsions as the book burning represents and can only be preserved by the self-sacrificing efforts of a few individuals. The individuals in this communal society literally give up their identities to become the books they have memorized: ironically, this new culture seems to care as little for the individual as the mass culture from which Montag has escaped. The difference is that the new society allows for a multiplicity of viewpoints and hence holds out some hope for the eventual revival of the human imagination.

Ray Bradbury's Childhood and Ancestors

Sam Weller

Sam Weller is a professor in the Fiction Writing Department at Columbia College Chicago and the authorized biographer of Ray Bradbury.

Bradbury has adamantly stood by his story that he recalls the traumatic events of his birth and circumcision. Whether or not Bradbury's early recollections span to his very beginnings, it is clear that his upbringing in Waukegan, Illinois, significantly shaped him. In this selection, Weller paints a picture of Bradbury's idyllic hometown and shares one of Bradbury's most colorful ancestral stories, about an accused witch in Salem. Weller relates that Bradbury's argument against censorship began centuries before his birth, with an unjust verdict against a long-ago ancestor.

> Ray Bradbury's most significant contribution to our culture is showing us that the imagination has no foreseeable boundaries. His skills as a storyteller have inspired and empowered generations to tell their stories no matter how bizarre or improbable. Today we need Ray Bradbury's gifts more than ever, and his stories have made him immortal.
>
> —*Steven Spielberg, Academy Award-winning director*

"**I** remember the day I was born."

With this Dickensian [like the work of nineteenth-century British novelist Charles Dickens] flourish, so begins the life story of Ray Bradbury. The birth recollection was one of Ray's

Sam Weller, "Remembrance of Things Past," in *The Bradbury Chronicles*. New York: William Morrow (An imprint of HarperCollins), 2005, pp. 11–28. Copyright © 2005 by Sam Weller. Reprinted by permission of HarperCollins Publishers.

favorite stories to tell. Not surprisingly, it often provoked audible incredulity from his audiences—whether one person or a room full of Bradbury devotees.

"I have what might be called almost total recall back to my birth," he continued. "This is a thing I have debated with psychologists and with friends over the years. They say, 'It's impossible.' Yet I remember."

This much is certain: Ray Douglas Bradbury arrived in the world, in Waukegan, Illinois, at 4:50 P.M. on August 22, 1920, with Dr. Charles Pierce presiding at Maternity Hospital, a few blocks west of the small Bradbury family home. Ray had overstayed his time in the womb by a month, and it was his theory that the additional incubation time may have heightened his senses. "When you stay in the womb for ten months, you develop your eyesight and your hearing. So when I was born, I remember it," he insisted. And who is to argue?

Bradbury's Earliest Memories

"Born to Mr. and Mrs. Leo Bradbury, 11 South St. James Street, a son," proclaimed the birth announcement in the *Waukegan Daily Sun*. Although the name on his birth certificate was spelled "*R-a-y*," Ray said he was originally given the name "Rae" after Rae Williams, a cousin on his father's side, and that it was not until the first grade that, at a teacher's recommendation, his parents changed the spelling of his first name. The name was too feminine, the teacher said, and the boy would be teased.

The origin of his middle name, however, is not in dispute. Ray's mother, a great cinema fan who would soon pass this love on to her son, chose his middle name, Douglas, for the swashbuckling screen star Douglas Fairbanks.

Of his birth, Ray claimed to remember "the camera angle" as he emerged into the world. He recalled the terrific pain of being born, the sensation of going from darkness to light, and the desperate desire to remain enshrouded in the shadowy realm of the womb. Lending further Freudian [related to psychoanalyst Sigmund Freud] fodder to skeptical developmental psychologists everywhere, Ray added, "I remember suckling, the taste of my mother's breast milk, and nightmares about being born experienced in my crib in the first weeks of my life."

Two days after the birth, Ray recalled his first encounter with real fear. His father wrapped him in a blanket and carried him into downtown Waukegan. They climbed a dark stairwell and entered a second-floor doctor's office. Ray remembered the bright, otherworldly light and the cold tiled room and what he would later realize was the scent of Lysol. He distinctly recalled the milk-white ghost face of a doctor holding a stainless steel scalpel. And then he felt the sharp pain of circumcision.

Many years later, a friend of Ray's, the author, critic, and editor of the *Magazine of Fantasy and Science Fiction*, Anthony Boucher, remarked that Ray Bradbury had a "back to the womb complex." Ray responded, with typical Bradburian aplomb, "Yes . . . but whose womb?"

The Origins of "Green Town"

The birthplace of Ray Bradbury, Waukegan, Illinois, is perched on the edge of a gently rising bluff that overlooks the slate-green waters of Lake Michigan. The city stands some forty miles north of downtown Chicago, as the raven flies. Centuries ago, this land was densely forested. Carved at the end of the ice age by melting glaciers that scored the soft heartland soil, it is marked by deep ravines that scar the landscape, eventually opening out into Lake Michigan. While the land to the west of the city is level farmland, Waukegan, with these dramatic, densely forested ravines, coldwater creeks, and the bluff the city stands on, offers a gentle contrast to the popular image of table-flat American heartland.

Today, Waukegan is a city at a crossroads. The turn-of-the-century grandeur of this lakefront community has given way to a long economic decline. In Ray's childhood, the Waukegan lakefront, with its sandy beaches, was a popular destination, vibrant and crowded with people. On warm summer days, it bloomed with colorful parasols, and men, women, and children swam in the cool lake. But decades passed and the crown jewel of Waukegan, its beachfront, shriveled under industry and pollution. Though the factories are mostly abandoned today, they still stand, like rust-laden skeletons on cold winter days as the winds gust in off Lake Michigan. Downtown Waukegan has also changed. Storefronts stand vacant; For Lease signs are propped up in many window displays. While some of the wealthiest suburbs in the nation are nestled on the lakefront between Waukegan and Chicago, Waukegan remains peculiar in its decaying isolation, an aging town with a rich history and the high hopes of future revitalization.

Ray Bradbury's connections to fantasy, space, cinema, to the macabre and the melancholy, were all born of his years spent running, jumping, galloping through the woods, across the fields, and down the brick-paved streets of Waukegan. His lifelong love of comics was born here, along with his connection to magic and his symbiotic relationship to Halloween. Although he moved away from the Midwest for good at the age of thirteen, Ray Bradbury is a prairie writer. The prairie is in his voice and it is his moral compass. It is his years spent in Waukegan, Illinois—later rechristened by Ray as "Green Town" in many books and stories—that forever shaped him.

A Place of Everlasting Inspiration

In his fiction, from *Something Wicked This Way Comes* to the semi-autobiographical *Dandelion Wine* and its unpublished sequel, *Farewell Summer*, Ray Bradbury would immortalize Waukegan as an idyllic slice of small-town Americana. And indeed, in the 1920s and 1930s it was idyllic. The barbershops, traveling carnivals, and electric trolley cars were all a part of daily life, as were the annual parades of aged American Civil War veterans marching through town. On summer days, there was the rustling of maple, oak, and elm—a canopy over the sun-dappled streets. There were corner drugstores and cigar shops with wooden Indians perched at their entrances. Ice-cream parlors with their snow-white marble tops and their thumping ceiling fans offered summer solace.

But as with most American towns, Waukegan was more than its apple-pie visage revealed. A city with a rich history, it had a palpable magic and a shadowy dark side—just like its native son, Ray Bradbury.

Peering beneath his hometown's romantic surface is paramount to understanding the mind of Ray Bradbury. It is as if the city of Waukegan, with uncanny prescience, had offered itself up as yet another metaphor for Ray's imagination. Indeed, the city's history is full of images and events that appear sewn through the subtle fabric of its most famous son's stories. . . .

Waukegan, in 1920, the year Ray Bradbury was born, was a booming city of 33,499 people. Some fans of the Green Town novels, *Dandelion Wine* and *Something Wicked This Way Comes*, find this number sizable; Waukegan was, in reality, much larger than Ray's fictionalization of small-town America. In 1920, the city was a bustling industrial town; the harbor was busy with Great Lakes ship traffic; and the American Steel and Wire Company, where Ray's maternal grandfather, Swedish-born Gustav Moberg, worked, was thriving. In the late summer of 1920, the beaches along Lake Michigan were a popular retreat, and often the Bradbury family spent their afternoons there. Genesee Street, with its whirling barber poles and storefront display windows, was picturesque Main Street USA. Peace and serenity presided over this slice of the Heartland. The First World War had ended victoriously. The country was at the dawn of the Jazz Age. Indeed, it was a good time and a good place to be born, and throughout his life, Ray Bradbury returned to Waukegan again and again for inspiration.

The Story of Bradbury's Ancestors

Certainly, the Bradbury family tree extended well beyond Waukegan, Illinois. Bradbury genealogical records document the family's history to the year 1433 in England. In 1634, Thomas Bradbury, born in 1610 in Wicken-Bonant, England, was the first in the family to cross the Atlantic and arrive in the colonies. He quickly became an influential member of his new community, serving as Deputy to the General Court and later as an associate judge. But it was Thomas's wife, Mary, who would make family history. On July 26, 1692, Mary Bradbury was summoned to the Salem Town courthouse: She was charged with witchcraft.

The seventy-two-year-old mother of eleven stood before the magistrate. How fearful this elderly woman must have been. "I am wholly innocent of any such wickedness through the goodness of god that have kept me hitherto," she proclaimed. But her plea fell on deaf ears.

Mary Bradbury—née Mary Perkins—was a prominent and respected resident of Salisbury, Massachusetts, in the county of Essex. In all, 118 members of the community signed a petition, testifying to her good character. Yet even with her reputation, the support of friends and neighbors, and her husband's influential position, she could not avoid the charge.

In 1692, a tempest of fear stormed through the Massachusetts Bay Colony, prompting what would become the infamous Salem Witch Trials. What began with two young girls experiencing convulsive seizures escalated into an unprecedented inquisition. From May to October 1692, nineteen convicted "witches" were put to death by hanging, one more was tortured, and at least five died while imprisoned; all told, at least 160 people were accused. The town of Salem was consumed by hysteria. A perceived malevolent outbreak of the "Evil Hand" had over-taken the colonial New England settlement and the townspeople would stop at nothing to rid themselves and their community of this curse.

A New American Witch Hunt

The charges against Mary Bradbury stemmed from wild allegations made by two men who, while walking by the Bradbury home, claimed to have seen a blue boar charge out of her yard's open gate. More people cited Mrs. Bradbury as responsible for an outbreak of sickness aboard a seafaring ship bound for Barbados; she had made the butter for the crew and, it was alleged, the butter had made the crew ill (never mind that refrigeration did not exist). A man testified to have seen Mrs. Bradbury aboard the ship. The weather had turned foul, he recalled, and there she was, in the moonlight, perched on the capstan of the vessel, an apparition portending doom.

With all this testimony leveled against her, on September 6, 1692, Mary Bradbury was found guilty and sentenced to die. But she escaped prison and the gallows. History presumes that, given her husband's prominence, guards were bribed, helping the woman escape execution. Mary Bradbury, convicted of witchcraft and sorcery during the Salem Witch Trials, died a free woman, at the age of eighty-five, on December 20, 1700.

More than 250 years after the tragedy at Salem, Mary's descendant Ray Bradbury would stand up against another set of incriminators and decry a new American witch hunt begun in the McCarthy era. How fitting that the man who wrote one of the quintessential works of anticensorship, a book that lambasted totalitarian rule, a book about government run amok, was a direct descendant of an accused Salem witch. In many ways, *Fahrenheit 451* can be read not only as a response to the McCarthy hearings, but as a centuries-old response from a long-lost relative.

An Interview with Ray Bradbury

Ray Bradbury, Interviewed by John Geirland

John Geirland is a frequent contributor to Wired *magazine and a coauthor of* Digital Babylon, *an informal history of Hollywood and the Internet.*

In this 1998 interview with Geirland, Ray Bradbury proves himself a skillful urban designer, even though he is weary of new technologies. Having never driven an automobile, Bradbury is an advocate of public transportation and believes all freeways should be demolished. Freeways destroy cities' ability to be what they should be, he says: places where people can get together, eat, shop, and have fun. Bradbury shares why he cannot understand people's obsessions with other modern "conveniences," such as the Internet, computers, and telephones.

Long before *Pathfinder* [*Mars Pathfinder*, later renamed the *Carl Sagan Memorial Station*, launched on December 4, 1996, by the National Aeronautics and Space Agency] rumbled across the rocky soil of Mars, Ray Bradbury owned the Red Planet in the popular imagination, courtesy of *The Martian Chronicles* (1950). His 600-plus short stories have laid claim to other worlds as well. "The Veldt" (1950) inspired a generation of smart-home and VR [virtual reality] pioneers. "A Sound of Thunder" (1952) illustrated chaos theory's butterfly effect years before the theory existed. And fireman Montag's dash for freedom, televised by pursuing helicopters in *Fahrenheit 451* (1953), could easily be on Fox's fall schedule. In fact, cameras are ready to roll on Mel Gibson's version of *Fahrenheit 451*, and Avon Books is reissuing many of the 78-year-old

John Geirland, "Bradbury's Tomorrowland," *Wired*, vol. 6, no. 10, October 1998. Copyright © 1998 by Conde Nast Publications Inc. Reproduced by permission of the author.

author's titles. The man who once said "Give me an ounce of fact and I will produce you a ton of theory by tea this afternoon" is also an urban design consultant; his ideas have contributed to Disney's Epcot [Center] and the revitalization of downtown Los Angeles. *Wired* asked Bradbury how far we've come from the future he wrote in the '50s.

Wired: Describe the city of the future.

Bradbury: Disneyland. They've done everything right: It has hundreds of trees and thousands of flowers they don't need, but which they put in anyway. It has fountains and places to sit. I've visited 30 or 40 times over the years, and there's very little I would change. Of course, Paris is where Walt Disney learned all of his lessons. I once called John Hench at Disney Imagineering: "John, for God's sake, I just noticed [French architect Eugène] Viollet-le-Duc's Notre-Dame spire on the side of Sleeping Beauty's castle."

"That's right," he said. "Walt put it there."

What other lessons can we take from the City of Light?

The secret of cities is the conviviality of food. Paris has 20,000 restaurants—if you build a city with 20,000 restaurants, you have a social city. The United States, and especially Los Angeles, has forgotten how to eat, how to dine. We need cities where people can meet, shop, and enjoy themselves. That's all cities are, and all they ever will be.

Eliminating Porches

You want to shut down LA's freeways. Is that practical?

We can eliminate cars and get back to public transit—I've lived in Los Angeles 64 years and I don't have a driver's license. Cars have destroyed cities. And the reason there's traffic on the freeway is because the freeway is there. Freeway driving has nothing to do with real business needs—it's an excuse for getting out of the office.

Once the freeways are gone, you propose to build 80 plazas throughout the LA area. What do you have in mind?

I created a blueprint for an ideal plaza—400 tables, a thousand chairs in the open, all kinds of restaurants surrounding it, and theaters at the four corners: a motion picture theater, a silent motion picture theater, a theater for dramatic presentations, and a music hall presenting all kinds of things, including symphonies and rock. You have to have a social mix.

How about using some of the space to build [American inventor and cofounder of Thinking Machines Corporation] Danny Hillis's 10,000-year clock? That would certainly get people thinking long-term.

He's completely wrong. You can't think of the future, because you're not going to be there.

Yet so much of your work has predicted the future.

Almost everything in *Fahrenheit 451* has come about, one way or the other—the influence of television, the rise of local TV news, the neglect of education. As a result, one area of our society is brainless. But I utilized those things in the novel because I was trying to *prevent* a future, not *predict* one.

The authorities in Fahrenheit 451 also eliminated porches to reduce social interaction. Has this come to pass?

It varies from territory to territory. I was in Omaha [Nebraska] recently and my God, the size of the lawns and porches and the feeling of community was incredible. We've been so busy building outside the city that the city centers are falling apart. Now we're building substitute cities, such as malls—a substitute for what we used to have in every downtown in America.

You Cannot Miss What You Have Never Had

How would you change the educational system?

The president [Bill Clinton] says he wants to wire [computers into] every schoolroom. I say it should happen in third grade maybe, but kindergarten through second grade has got to be educating kids to read and write, otherwise they can't

In 2002 Ray Bradbury received a star on the Hollywood Walk of Fame for his contributions to films, television, and literature. Vince Bucci/Stringer/Getty Images.

use the tools. Get education back on a local level where it's controlled by teachers, parents, and students. What do governments know about education? Nothing.

Somewhere in a third-grade class there is a 9-year-old who will be walking on Mars in 2020. How should we prepare that kid?

We already are, my fellow writers and myself. [Franco-German humanitarian] Albert Schweitzer said do something wonderful, people may imitate it. If you dream the proper dreams, and share the myths with people, they will want to grow up to be like you. All the astronauts I meet tell me they have been influenced by me to grow up the way they did. If you and I dream properly and creatively, then the future will be secured. But reality will kill you unless you deal with it through myths and metaphors. The trouble with people who write realistically is that they want to electrocute you.

What myths should we share?

Space travel is our final, greatest dream. If we can reach the nearest solar system, then we can live for an extra million years. But ultimately, the particular myth is not important— it's how to fall and stay in love. Teach students to be in love with life, to love their work, to create at the top of their lungs. I love what I'm doing and started loving it when I was 12. Find something to love when you're young—archeology, mythology, Egyptology, even computerology—then you can change the future.

Are PCs and the Net making the future friendlier for community?

No, you've got to make personal contact. Go to the library and build a network of personal friends, a half dozen or so, as I've done over the years with other writers. Stop talking on the telephone, stop talking on the stupid Internet. It's a waste of time.

So, no Internet, no computer, not even a driver's license. Is the modern world passing you by?

You don't miss what you've never had. People talk about sex when you're 12 years old and you don't know what they're talking about—I don't know what people are talking about when they talk about driving. I grew up with roller skates, a bicycle, using the trolley and bus lines until they went out of existence. No, you don't miss things. Put me in a room with a pad and a pencil and set me up against a hundred people with a hundred computers—I'll outcreate every goddamn sonofabitch in the room.

CHAPTER 2

Fahrenheit 451
and Censorship

The Timeliness of Ray Bradbury's Criticism of Censorship

Edward E. Eller

Edward E. Eller is an assistant professor in the Department of English at the University of Louisiana at Monroe and the department's director of technology.

Ray Bradbury wrote Fahrenheit 451 *during a time when Americans were growing increasingly concerned that communism might take over and rob them of their rights. This period followed World War II, a war fought to end Nazism; among the atrocities of Germany's leader Adolf Hitler was his extreme censorship and burning of books. In this viewpoint, Eller points out how, through* Fahrenheit 451, *Bradbury underscores the hypocrisy of the 1950s censorship movement led by Senator Joseph McCarthy.* Fahrenheit's *fireman Montag can only escape the confinement of his culture through the very books he is paid to burn.*

Bradbury developed *Fahrenheit 451* during the late 1940s and published it in 1950 [1953], just after World War II and during America's growing fear of communism. During World War II, Hitler and the Nazis had banned and burned hundreds of thousands of books. However, the Nazis went further; using new technologies, they attempted one of the largest mind control experiments in history by setting up state controlled schools and a propaganda machine which censored all ideas and information in the public media. To make matters worse, after the war the Soviet Union developed its own propaganda machine, created an atomic bomb, and invaded

Edward E. Eller, "An Overview of *Fahrenheit 451*," *Literature Resource Center*. Detroit: Gale, 2010. Copyright © Gale, a part of Cengage Learning, Inc. Reproduced by permission.

Eastern Europe. All this time, new technological innovations allowed these fascist states to more effectively destroy the books they didn't find agreeable and produce new forms of communication implanted with state-sanctioned ideas.

Finally, and most significantly for Bradbury, the U.S. government responded to its fear of growing communist influence with attempts to censor the media and its productions, including literature. In other words, it responded with the same tactics of tyranny implemented by Nazi Germany and the Soviet Union. The McCarthy hearings in the early fifties attempted to rein in what it saw as communist sympathies among authors and Hollywood producers. The FBI investigated the *potential* disloyalty of U.S. citizens. The federal government began attempts to restrict the free speech of judges and university professors by requiring loyalty oaths. *Fahrenheit 451* appeared in this political climate of technologically supported suspicion and censorship, a climate which seemed to promise the possibility of the mass conformity in our citizenry. It is no surprise, then, that these concerns are central to the book's themes.

People as Machines

Montag and his wife, Mildred, live in what Bradbury imagines as the culture which might be produced if such trends continued. They live in a futuristic community that uses technology to control what they think and feel by controlling what they see and hear. They are encouraged to use sedatives to keep themselves docile and their senses dull. They have all the latest entertainment technology—three walls of their "living room" display soap operas, "seashell thimble" radios pump high fidelity sound directly into their ears, and two-hundred-foot billboards line the freeway, blocking out the natural landscape and replacing it with advertisements. There is one telling scene in which Montag attempts to read and remember the *Book of Ecclesiastes* while riding on the train to see Faber, his newfound teacher. He cannot, however, manage it because the train's sound system plays an advertisement for Denham's Dentifrice over and over: "Denham's does it" with a bouncy jingle that interferes with his ability to think and remember. Everywhere he goes in these controlled spaces the system is there to limit and shape what he thinks by feeding him sights and sounds.

Mildred is the end product of this system. Mildred, as does most of the community, immerses herself in the media provided for her to consume. Whenever she is not at the TV, she plugs in her earphones, always soaking up the artificial stimulus and messages someone else feeds to her. The result is that she is literally incapable of thought and remembering. When Montag questions her about an argument that the characters are having on the wall TV, she can't remember what it was about even though it happened only one minute past. When he is sick and asks Mildred to get him some aspirin, she leaves the room and then wanders back a few minutes later, not a thought in her head.

The situation is so serious for Mildred that she might as well be an empty shell, a corpse, or a machine herself. As it turns out, Mildred is literally on the verge of being a corpse, having almost overdosed on sedatives. Montag comes home after a satisfying book-burning, only to find that his house feels like a "mausoleum" and his wife "cold" and himself "with the feeling of a man who will die in the next hour for lack of air." The oppressive atmosphere of death and emptiness is aggravated by the visit of the hospital "technicians" who come to the house to service Mildred. They treat her like an extension of the snakelike machine they use to "take out the old and put in the new." He finds out that they act as casually as "handymen" doing a fix-it-up job because they clean out nine to ten stomachs a night. In other words, people are no more than extensions of machines; they are machines themselves. The "technicians" treat them appropriately, as either broken, like Mildred, or in good repair. Technology violates their humanity.

The most complete violation of humanity would be the replacement of the human with a machine in perfect conformity with the system which created it. This may not be possible with humans, but it makes the Mechanical Hound the perfect creature of the system. It makes the Hound a fail-safe against the possibility that a human member of the mass society will be tainted by individuality and independent thought. The Hound cannot be so tainted. It lacks the two key ingredients which might allow it individuality and independence—its own thoughts and true sensations. As Beatty says, "It doesn't think anything we don't want it to think . . . a fine bit of craftsmanship." Later, Montag describes it as a thing in the world which "cannot touch the world." It lacks the mind of its own and body that feels. This makes the Hound the best guardian of their way of life. As a result, when Montag grows more aware of how the system has deprived him of sensation and thought, the Hound grows more aware of Montag. The Hound may not be able to touch the world, but it recognizes the smell of thought, it recognizes that Montag does not belong to the same system it does.

Montag's Teachers

All is not lost, though. Montag's teachers lead him out of this controlled and sterile world. Clarisse, the young seventeen-year-old "oddball," is his first teacher. Clarisse prods him back into experiencing the outside world's sensations, especially smells as simple as "apricots" and "strawberries," "old leaves" and "cinnamon," smells which up to now have always been dominated by the odor of kerosene. She entices him out of the insulated "walls" of their house and into the rain, away from the rule books and 3-D comics whose content is strictly controlled so as to ensure that everything is agreeable—that

In this still from the 1966 film adaptation of Ray Bradbury's novel Fahrenheit 451, *fireman Guy Montag (right, played by Oskar Werner) burns books.* Copyright © 2010 Alamy Ltd. All rights reserved.

is, all packaged to promote conformity and consumerism. She ignores his authority by openly questioning whether he can even think and challenges his smug superiority by seeing through his "mask" of happiness and into his deeper discontent. She tells him how she eavesdrops on others and finds that young "people don't talk about anything" except to trade the brand names of clothes and cars. She points out that the two-hundred-foot billboards hide the real world. She teaches him that he and everyone else are subject to the dictates of others, that their thoughts and experiences are controlled.

When Clarisse "disappears," Captain Beatty, Montag's superior, ironically becomes his "teacher." Even though Beatty's purpose is to bring Montag back into conformity with the system, he drives Montag farther away during his "history lesson" on the origins and purpose of the firemen book-burners. Beatty tells him that the condition of the world and the rejection of "books" and their ideas was a "mass" phenomenon. Not only did the population find it easier to read condensed versions of literature and digests rather than whole works, but it was also more "agreeable." Books are notorious for their slippery and contradictory ideas. It becomes easier and safer to do away with them altogether; this is the job of the fireman. Over time, substitutions displaced books altogether: photography and film, rule books, sports, and trivial information. Fill them up with "non-combustible" stuff so they feel "absolutely brilliant" but lack any thought which may have "two sides . . . no philosophy or sociology," says Beatty. Then we can have a perfect tyranny of technology over the comfortable and thoughtless. The problem, however, is that if books are the way to "melancholy" and unhappiness, then why is Mildred so deeply depressed and Montag so angry?

Montag's third "teacher" explains the source of their unhappiness. Faber, the old college English teacher, argues that the "telivisor" is irresistible. Furthermore, if you "drop a seed" (take a sedative) and turn on the televisor, "[It] grows you any shape it wishes. It *becomes* and *is* the truth." It makes a people into what it wants them to be, a conforming mass all acting in unison. Perhaps the most frightening image in the book makes this idea of thoughtless masses under the direction of technology concrete for us. At the end of the chase scene when the Mechanical Hound closes in and Montag approaches the river, the broadcaster asks the whole population to rise and go to the door and everybody look out at the street at the same time. Montag has a vision of the population acting in near perfect unison under the direction of a technological device—a truly frightening vision of humans turned into conforming automatons.

Escaping the Technological Cocoon

Faber argues, however, that books have a "quality" or "texture of information." Books have a depth of imaginative experience and completeness of information which the media soaps lack. This "texture of information," along with the leisure time to absorb it and the freedom to act on what it allows us to discover, is what Montag needs to make him, if not happy, then at least satisfied. In a sense, Montag's awakening sensations, his growing awareness of smells other than kerosene, his new appreciation for rain and the light of the moon, symbolize the "quality" found in books. Throughout the book, we get hints about this. After his wife's mishap with the sedatives, he feels suffocated and empty, and in a fit of desire for something more, he throws the sealed windows of the bedroom to let the moon's light fill the room. When he is trying to memorize the *Book of Ecclesiastes* and the Denham's Dentifrice advertisement interferes, he has this urge to run out of the train and experience anything, any sensation, even if it's the pain of a pounding heart and lungs gasping for air. When he lay in his bed the night of the old woman's burning, he feels that he "never ... quite ... touched ... anything." Parallel to his yearning for the "texture of information" in books, he has a yearning for deeper and richer bodily experiences and sensations.

All in all, the idea is that if Montag is to escape the technological cocoon which the culture has built up around him, he must do it in mind and body, in books and sensations. This is no new idea, that the mind and body are one. If this is true, then it is also true that if you control the experiences of the body so, too, will the mind be controlled. And vice-versa, if you control the depth of ideas and smooth out the "texture of information" in the media, the body will lose its ability to absorb a wide range of sensation. We see this effect on Montag when he finally climbs up out of the river. Having been deprived of deep and textured sensations most of his life, he was "crushed" by the "tidal wave of smell and sound." He experiences an onslaught of odor: musk, cardamom, ragweed, moss, blood, cloves, and warm dust. The narrator tells us, "enough to feed on for a lifetime. . . . lakes of smelling and feeling and touching."

It is both the mind and the body of the population which the prevailing union of politics and technology has repressed in Montag's culture. The book people Montag discovers at the end of the novel show that you must abandon the system and get "outside" the technological cocoon. You must internalize the conflicting, richly textured information and ideas of books before you can be an individual not subject to the repressive conformity of the masses. The book people are literally outside in nature as well as figuratively outsiders alienated from the culture. They have literally internalized books as well as figuratively become "book covers." They have brought the book and the body, thought and sensation together. Maybe this is why Bradbury was so outraged by the book burnings in Nazi Germany. Maybe this is why he says "that when Hitler burned a book I felt it as keenly, please forgive me, as his killing a human, for in the long sum of history they are one and the same flesh."

The Dictatorship of American Censorship

Erika Gottlieb

Before her death in 2007, Erika Gottlieb taught English litera-
ture at several Canadian universities, including McGill Univer-
sity in Montreal.

In this selection Gottlieb examines Ray Bradbury's perspectives
on culture in Fahrenheit 451. *While the book calls attention to*
dictatorship and other social and political repressions, Bradbury
focuses his story on cultural and intellectual repression. By con-
centrating on book burning, he reveals how a society can sup-
press itself, even without the aid of a dictator. As Chief Beatty
tells Montag in Fahrenheit, *government did not ban books; in-*
stead, technology and easy entertainment eventually squeezed
books out of society. In the end, claims Beatty, people were hap-
pier without books. Published during the media-controlled 1950s,
Bradbury was prophesying a gloomy future for the masses.

In Bradbury's *Fahrenheit 451* the terms of injustice are dic-
tated by a government that rules through firemen who do
not put out fires but burn books, set houses on fire, and, like
[Eugene] Zamiatin's "guardians" or [George] Orwell's Thought
Police, spy upon people and urge them to report on subversive elements. The story takes place in the United States some
time in the future. In order to have a stable society, the government uses the anti-intellectual argument that reading is
conducive to critical thinking, and thinking creates unrest and
disorder—in other words, psychological and social instability.

Bradbury's plot line is strongly reminiscent of Orwell's in
Nineteen Eighty-four: fireman Guy Montag, a man in a privi-

Erika Gottlieb, "Dictatorship Without a Mask: Bradbury's *Fahrenheit 451*, Vonnegut's *Player Piano*, and Atwood's *The Handmaid's Tale*," in *Dystopian Fiction East and West.* McGill-Queen's University Press, 2001, pp. 88–95. Copyright © 2001 McGill-Queen's University Press. All rights reserved. Reproduced by permission.

leged position, is suddenly awakened, by the love of a young woman, to dissatisfaction with his life in the oppressive system. It is the young woman's contrast to Montag's wife, Mildred, a complacent product of the system who spends her days watching the three wall size television screens in her living room, that makes Montag awaken to a light buried within him. The young girl's name is Clarisse, and appropriately she clarifies Montag's subconscious thoughts for him: "How like a mirror, too, her face. Impossible; for how many people did you know that refracted your own light to you?".

Awakened to a sense of his unhappiness and the oppressive nature of the political system, Guy Montag gradually also finds himself in conflict with the firemen's perceptions of justice. In the course of his work he is in a position to hide away some books; he starts to read them with increasing fascination, and for this offence he eventually faces the gravest punishment. Even if he is not expected formally to stand public trial, his trial is nevertheless extremely important for the structure of the book: he is "tried" in a series of seemingly casual interrogations by the Firechief, Captain Beatty, who also happens to open for him the traditional "window on history" by explaining how the firemen came to power as a result of the decline of book learning, the public acceptance of censorship, and the seductive power of the media in the United States of the early 1950s.

After his "trial in installments," Montag is not even told that he has been found guilty and condemned. Beatty simply orders his subordinate to join him on the fire truck on its way to the daily task of setting a subversive's house on fire. It is only when they arrive that Montag recognizes whose house he is expected to burn down: "Why," said Montag slowly, "we've stopped in front of my house".

Without laying charges or providing evidence, Beatty lets the trial take its final stage: the meting out of justice. As a fireman Montag is to carry out his own sentence, just as he has been carrying out the sentence on others who have been found guilty. At this point, however, Montag takes justice into his own hands: instead of setting his house on fire, he turns the flame thrower against Firechief Beatty, kills him, and then runs for his life. . . . Montag gets away with his rebellion against the system; he escapes and takes shelter among the Book People, a subversive group whose members have memorized entire books to save the heritage of humanity.

Like Zamiatin's, [Aldous] Huxley's, and Orwell's dystopias, *Fahrenheit 451* is a society that denies its past; it has no records of past events, no books, no documents, and as a result, no framework for personal memory. However, unlike Huxley and Orwell, Bradbury does not represent the burning of books and the persecution of writers and readers as an *effect* of political dictatorship; rather, he creates a society that became a dictatorship *as a result of* burning books and discarding the classics of our civilization, all records of the past, indeed anything conducive to the development of personal memory and the working of the imagination. No doubt, Bradbury borrows elements from [Nazi leader Adolf] Hitler's and [former leader of the Soviet Union Joseph] Stalin's dictatorships. For example, it is Montag's wife who denounces him to Firechief Beatty; according to the laws established by both Hitler's and Stalin's dictatorships, a citizen's loyalty to the government should take precedence over loyalty to a spouse. Signs of dictatorial terror and violence are clearly discernible: subversives suspected of being critical of the system are quietly eliminated; children are taught to be obedient to the state but are encouraged to commit violence and risk their own lives and those of others by reckless driving and fighting. Bradbury's point is that this behaviour is natural in a society where people are bored and dislocated by the mental poverty that follows from lack of reading. Most significantly, and Bradbury suggests this to be the source of all its evils, this society burns books, just as Hitler did. Often what begins as the burning of a few books and the house where these have been found turns into a real *auto-da-fé*, a religious ritual of human sacrifice, as in the case of the old woman who decides to remain in her house and die with her books. She dies like a martyr, reciting the parting words of [clergyman and martyr] Hugh Latimer, burnt at the stake and martyred for his faith in 1555.

The old woman's trial and execution has a profound effect on Montag, completing the process begun by his meeting with Clarisse, the wish for radical change in himself and in society. While the Mechanical Hound, a deadly machine capable of detecting books and readers, is already sniffing at the Montags' door, Guy Montag is trying to explain his transformation to his wife: "That woman the other night ... You didn't see her face. And Clarisse. You never talked to her ... But I kept putting her alongside the firemen in the House last night, and I suddenly realized I didn't like them at all, and I didn't like myself at all any more".

The burning of books is not just the central but the only phenomenon Bradbury is interested in when describing how the entire political process of the United States could be moving towards a police state. In his 1966 introduction, written fifteen years after the novel, Bradbury states that he feared that the McCarthy era [led by Senator Joseph McCarthy], with its anti-intellectualism, censorship, and its encouragement of citizens' denunciations of one another, could introduce in the United States a society very much like Hitler's Germany or Stalin's Soviet Union. In commenting on the movie version that François Truffaut made of the novel, Bradbury sheds further light on the love of books as his central theme, and maybe also on the rather two-dimensional characterization that is more appropriate to an allegory than to a novel aiming for psychological verisimilitude. He congratulates Truffaut for capturing "the soul and the essence of the book," which is "the love story of, not a man and a woman, but a man and a library, a man and a book. An incredible love story indeed in this day when libraries, once more, are burning across the world."

By the end of the novel the burning of books can be recognized as the prefiguration of the approaching Apocalypse, the final war that may destroy our civilization. What Bradbury focuses on is one particular aspect of a police state, namely the repression of free speech, free thought, free press, the freedom of the imagination. He also draws attention to the power of the media not only to lie but also to fake events as a means of state propaganda. When Montag escapes without a trace, the crew of the television newscast improvises a scene where a man, chosen at random and photographed from a distance, is shot on the spot in order to convince viewers that "justice" has been served; the subversive has been instantly eliminated.

Ultimately Bradbury regards the suppression of truth as virtually the only, the core crime of totalitarian dictatorships, from which all other crimes follow. He tells us that "when Hitler burned a book, I felt it as keenly, please forgive me, as killing a human, for in the long sum of history, they are one and the same flesh." And he completes the thought: "Mind or body, put to the oven, is a sinful practice, and I carried this with me as I passed countless firehouses."

The narrower scope of his criticism notwithstanding, Bradbury follows the traditional strategies of dystopian satire, which asks the reader to examine the social pathologies of the present that could lead to the nightmare world in the future. In fact, Bradbury makes a concentrated effort to open for Montag "a window on history" that will clarify for the reader the satirist's targets by having both Firechief Beatty and Faber describe the past, the fifties—the time when the novel was written. Faber, a former English professor and a friend of Montag, points at the past, regretting that in the 1950s the humanities started to atrophy, began slowly to be destroyed in the name of the machine civilization. Students at universities abandoned courses in literature; *Readers' Digest* reduced classics to a quick, superficial one page read; and it became such a sensitive political issue to write about minorities or various ethnic groups that publishers gave up on publishing literature, and cheap works on sex and violence pushed out the classics to please the masses. Faber calls this process "the tyranny of the majority," a false egalitarianism that reduces everyone to the lowest common denominator, making Americans willing to give up what [English writer] Matthew Arnold would have called the best and most beautiful voices of humanity in the name of efficiency and saving time. Bradbury suggests that the American public of the fifties is responsible for the new regime. "Remember, the firemen are rarely necessary. The public itself stopped reading of its own accord". The political change, then, was not violent; it was simply the aftermath of cultural decline: "And then the Government, seeing how advantageous it was to have people reading only about passionate lips and the fist in the stomach, circled the situation with your fireeaters".

Intellectual as a Swear Word

While Faber's description of the sins of the fifties becomes a lament over the decline of book-learning, Montag's boss, Firechief Beatty, describes the same process as the rise of the media, and with it, the triumphant rise of the police state. A representative of dictatorial power, Beatty celebrates the firemen's reign, although he fails to explain how and why the firemen came to power and what motivates them to stay in power. In most general terms, of course, the Firechief reproduces the Grand Inquisitor's explanation of the happiness and stability the masses would enjoy at the price of accepting limitations on their freedom. Instead of turning directly on the heretic, the Grand Inquisitor [a character in Fyodor Dostoyevsky's *The Brothers Karamazov*] here admits his anti-intellectualism: "the word 'intellectual,' of course, became the swear word it deserved to be. You always dread the unfamiliar".

What for the Grand Inquisitor was the happiness of the masses is for Beatty the economic well being of the market. But the conclusion is the same: the masses should be protected from the burden of thinking for themselves: "the bigger your market, Montag, the less you handle controversy . . . Authors, full of evil thoughts, lock up your typewriters. They did. Magazines became a nice blend of vanilla tapioca . . . No wonder books stopped selling . . . comic books . . . three-dimensional sex magazines . . . It didn't come from the Government down. There was no dictum, no declaration, no censorship, to start with, no! Technology, mass exploitation, and minority pressure carried the trick, thank God! Today, thanks to them, you can stay happy all the time".

Beatty's speech recalls the self-justification of the Grand Inquisitor, who is convinced that by subverting the original spirit of Christ he can make the people "happy." However, Beatty's agenda does not explain exactly what that original spirit was that became subverted by the "Happiness boys" who forbade reading. Is it the original spirit of democracy? Then why did this spirit weaken in the fifties? "If you don't want a man unhappy politically, don't give him two sides to a question to worry him; give him one. Better yet, give him none. Let him forget there is such a thing as war. If the government is inefficient, top-heavy, and tax-mad, better it be all those than that people worry over it. Peace, Montag. Give the people contest . . . cram them full of noncombustible data. Then they'll feel they're thinking, they'll get a sense of motion without moving. And they'll be happy, because facts of that sort don't change".

The Rebirth of Civilization

Justifying the power of the firemen, Captain Beatty is like the high priest of the state religion, the only person who still knows the forbidden lore of the past. He is able to quote from the books he has burnt in his long years of service, and there is also an indication that, by giving up his love for reading in order to serve the anti-intellectual government, he made a sacrifice. . . . Yet Beatty cannot fully justify this sacrifice to himself and is consequently an unhappy man. Montag recognizes this suddenly when he is already on the run and recalls the circumstances of his trial and punishment. He cries out, "Beatty wanted to die!" He must have been tired of life when he exposed himself to the flame-thrower in Montag's hands.

Beatty is an ambiguous character: in the course of Montag's gradual conversion to book reading, Beatty gives several signs that he is fully aware of Montag's thoughts and feelings, including his fear of the Mechanical Hound. Beatty's personal visit to Montag's house when the latter stays home from work is also an ambiguous episode: it combines the possibilities that Beatty has come to spy on his subordinate, to carry on a pre-trial investigation, or to offer a friendly warning in his parting words to Montag: "Be well and stay well". Still, Beatty's consistent analysis of the world of the 1950s that led to the world of *Fahrenheit 451* indicates that as Ideal Readers we should be careful about censorship, the atrophy of book-reading, and the media's unchecked rise to power if we wish to stop a decline that may lead to a destructive total war in which "our civilization is flinging itself to pieces". . . .

Guy Montag manages to kill the "high priest" or Grand Inquisitor of the system and escape. Behind him the city is being destroyed by the war, but Guy Montag finds a chance for survival in the country among a group of bibliophiles [book lovers] who memorize entire books to make sure their words will not be forgotten. It is from these words, Bradbury suggests, that our civilization may be reborn, like the phoenix who "everytime he burnt himself up . . . sprang out of the ashes . . . born all over again".

Although [critic] Jack Zipes has reason to say that "throughout the novel, war lurks in the background until it finally erupts," there is little evidence that "the obvious reference here is to the Cold War and the Korean War which might lead to such an atomic explosion as that which occurs at the end of the book." In fact, when Beatty opens the "window on history" for Montag, describing to him the problems in the fifties that precipitated the reign of the book-burning firemen, he does not refer to any specific war. The story suggests that when "our civilization is flinging itself to pieces" and when it is "born all over again" as a phoenix, both the destruction and the rebirth of the world are connected exclusively with the elimination or the survival of books. The reader may well find that the equation of the decline of book-reading with the increased chances of the world's destruction by nuclear war is not sufficiently convincing. The novel reads more like a parable about the importance of book-learning and of assuring the survival of our cultural heritage than a convincing political analysis of a society on its way to the dystopia of dictatorship and destruction.

One of Bradbury's critics objects to the naïveté of Bradbury's political analysis, claiming that, "Bradbury does not locate the source of destruction in the state, class society, or technology, but in humankind himself." In itself, I do not believe that drawing attention to the complicity of the masses in allowing the emergence of the dictator is a sign of political naïveté. If we recall Frigyes Karinthy's "Barrabbas," or Hannah Arendt's political analysis of this phenomenon, the question of why the people would opt for the dictator is a question well worth asking. The problem in Bradbury's analysis of dictatorship is rather that we do not see the clear connection between the people's desire for "happiness" and the ways the government seduces them to follow its own agenda. Except for trying to stay in power, the government in this dystopic society has no agenda, no program, not even a program to fabricate its own self-justification.

In concentrating on book-burning, Bradbury chooses one element he finds most frightening in totalitarian systems and works on that theme, as it were in isolation, to show how the United States could also turn into a dictatorship like societies in Eastern and Central Europe. As a political critique of a society on its way to totalitarianism the book is not quite convincing. But *Fahrenheit 451* is probably less a full-fledged political dystopia than the diagnosis of a new cultural phenomenon that [Canadian philosopher and English professor] Marshall McLuhan explored in *The Gutenberg Galaxy* (1962) [in which McLuhan analyzes the effects of mass media], foreshadowed by *The Mechanical Bride* (1951) [in which McLuhan investigates popular culture]. With open fascination McLuhan follows the passing away of a civilization based on the printed word, on reading and writing. Reading McLuhan, it seems that the old world is stepping aside and saluting the rise to power of a new world created by the electronic media, in the character of a rather absent minded new dictator not yet entirely set on either a benign or a malignant course. Yet it is a dictator when it dictates new terms to our perceptions, modes of thinking, political discourse, until "the medium [becomes our] message." Unlike McLuhan, Bradbury responds to this phenomenon by expressing the moral apprehension of the humanist. Not quite a convincing dystopian critique of the dangers of a totalitarian political system or a police state, the novel is a memorable and passionate outcry against the cultural losses implied by the passing away of book culture in the media-controlled consumer society of the 1950s.

The Cold War
and *Fahrenheit 451*

Kevin Hoskinson

Kevin Hoskinson teaches English at Lorain County Community College in Ohio.

In this article Hoskinson discusses Fahrenheit 451's *connections to the historical period in which it was written and published. This history included the Cold War, McCarthyism, and the development of the atomic bomb. The censorship enforced by the book's firemen ran parallel to the censorship endured by Americans living in the 1950s: both were fear-based and represented a divided sense of humanity. Still, through* Fahrenheit 451, *Ray Bradbury conveyed optimism for society and for the human spirit. Ultimately, Bradbury's book might have helped prevent the future society's embracing of the Cold War mentality.*

In a discussion . . . with interviewer David Mogen in 1980, Ray Bradbury stated, "*The Martian Chronicles* and *Fahrenheit 451* come from the same period in my life, when I was warning people. I was preventing futures". In this pairing of the two books, Bradbury suggests a deep kinship between the pieces and indicates the probability that they are more than just successive novels in his overall body of work. Though the two fictions are usually read as separate entities, if read as complementary works, they provide a more comprehensive view of a larger whole. As consecutive arrivals in Bradbury's postwar publications, and in their mutual attraction to similar major themes of the cold war era, *The Martian Chronicles* and *Fahrenheit 451* distinguish themselves as Bradbury's "cold war novels." . . .

Kevin Hoskinson, "*The Martian Chronicles* and *Fahrenheit 451*: Ray Bradbury's Cold War novels," *Extrapolation*, vol. 36, 1995. Copyright © 1995 by The Kent State University Press. Reproduced by permission.

[Bradbury's] *The Martian Chronicles* and *Fahrenheit 451* share a distinction as "cold war fiction" because in them, much more deliberately than in earlier or later publications, Bradbury deals with subjects and issues that were shaped by the political climate of the United States in the decade immediately following World War II. A number of significant events during these years transformed the character of America from a supremely confident, Nazi-demolishing world leader to a country with deep insecurities, one suddenly suspicious and vigilant of Communist activity within its citizenry. First, Joseph Stalin's immediate and unchecked occupation of Eastern European countries at the close of World War II left many Americans wondering if the United States and the [Franklin D.] Roosevelt administration hadn't foolishly misjudged Soviet intentions at the Yalta Conference in 1945. Second, the Soviet Union's subsequent acquisition of atomic weapons technology by 1949 would reinforce this position; it would also end the U.S. monopoly on thermonuclear weapons and raise questions about Communist agents in high-level government positions. Third, Senator Joseph McCarthy's public accusations of Communist activity in the State Department in 1950 (together with the inflammatory tactics of J. Edgar Hoover, the FBI, and a host of other right-wing government agencies) planted seeds of paranoia and subversion in the American culture that would blossom into fear and irrationality throughout the 1950s. As David Halberstam [American Pulitzer Prize–winning journalist and author known for his early work on the Vietnam War] points out, "It was a mean time. The nation was ready for witch-hunts". Through his examination of government oppression of the individual, the hazards of an atomic age, recivilization of society, and the divided nature of the "Cold War Man," Ray Bradbury uses *The Martian Chronicles* and *Fahrenheit 451* to expose the "meanness" of the cold war years.

During the [President Harry S.] Truman years of the early cold war, when the administration attempted to reverse the image of the Democratic party as being "soft" on communism, the U.S. government attempted to silence individuals who were thought to be "potentially disloyal" through various offices such as the Justice Department and the Loyalty Review Board. Truman himself released a press statement in July 1950 that granted authority over national security matters to the FBI. The statement expressed grave concern over "the Godless Communist Cause" and further warned that "it is important to learn to know the enemies of the American way of life". For Bradbury, such government-supported conformism amounted to censorship and ultimately led to the fostering of what [literary critic] William F. Touponce labels "mass culture" and what [English novelist] Kingsley Amis calls "conformist hell". We see Bradbury's strong distrust of "majority-held" views and official doctrine positions in several places in *The Martian Chronicles*; these areas of distrust, moreover, recur in *Fahrenheit 451*. . . .

Montag's Transformation

In *Fahrenheit 451* Bradbury [pursues an] attack on government-based censorship. . . . Set on Earth rather than on Mars, this novel follows the metamorphosis of Guy Montag, a fireman (a starter of fires in this future dystopian society) who comes to question and break free of the government that employs him to burn books. The novel opens with Montag having just returned to the firehouse after igniting another residence, "grinn[ing] the fierce grin of all men singed and driven back by flame". He is clearly of the majority at this point, loyal to his job and proud of wearing the salamander and the phoenix disc, the official insignia of the Firemen of America. But seventeen-year-old Clarisse McClellan, who is dangerous in Beatty's eyes because "she [doesn't] want to know how a thing [is] done, but why", points out some disturbing facts that Montag cannot escape: he answers her questions quickly with-

Director François Truffaut (right) instructs actors Julie Christie (middle) and Oskar Werner (left) during the filming of Fahrenheit 451, *based on Ray Bradbury's novel of the same name.* © Interfoto/Alamy.

out thinking; he can't remember if he knew there was dew on early-morning grass or not; he can't answer the question of whether he is happy or not. A growing unrest with his own lack of individual sensibilities creeps into Montag at Clarisse's challenges. As [literary critic] Donald Watt observes, Clarisse is "catalytic" and "dominant in Montag's growth to awareness", her role for Montag [is in], planting the seed of doubt that enacts a process of critical self-examination. These doubts about the government he is serving accumulate through the latest suicide attempt by Montag's wife, Mildred (and her casual acceptance of this attempt after she is resuscitated); through his witnessing of a book-hoarding woman who chose to ignite her own home rather than flee in the face of the firemen's flamethrowers; through the government's systematic elimination of Clarisse; through his own growing need to read and understand books.

Montag ultimately realizes that he cannot return to the firehouse. At this point he rejects both the realm of the majority and his association with Chief Beatty, who professes to "stand against the small tide of those who want to make everyone unhappy with conflicting theory and thought". Montag's liberation from the Firemen of America is augmented when he locates Faber (a former English professor and current member of the book-preserving underground), who offers Montag moral counsel and employs him as an infiltrator at the firehouse. Mildred, in the meantime, breaks her silence and sounds a fire alarm at the Montag residence. In a dramatic confrontation of Individual vs. State, Montag refuses Beatty's orders to burn his own house and instead turns the flamethrower on Beatty. This revolt severs Montag from the majority permanently; he then joins the underground movement to preserve books for the future as global war descends on the city.

The Theme of Human Precariousness

Another theme of the cold war years Bradbury takes up . . . is the precariousness of human existence in an atomic age. The eventual "success" of the Manhattan Project in 1945, which resulted in the development of the atomic bomb, came about only after several years' worth of blind groping toward the right physics equations by some of the brightest physicists in the world. The scientists were literally guessing about how to detonate the bomb, how big to make the bomb, and, most significantly, how strong the bomb would be. The project itself, in the words of [author] Lansing Lamont, was "a bit like trying to manufacture a new automobile with no opportunity to test the engine beforehand".

After studying various reports on a wide range of explosions in known history, the Los Alamos physicists determined that the atom bomb's force would fall somewhere in between the volcanic eruption of Krakatau in 1883 (which killed 36,000 people and was heard 3,000 miles away) and the 1917 explosion of the munitions ship Mont Blanc in Halifax Harbor, Nova Scotia (killing 1,100)—"hopefully a lot closer to Halifax," Lamont notes, "but just where [the scientists] couldn't be sure". The subsequent explosions at Hiroshima and Nagasaki made Americans more "sure" of the bomb's potential but not sure at all about whether the knowledge of its potential was worth the price of having created it in the first place. As a line of military defense against the spread of nazism, the bomb became a prime example of how science unleashed can, according to [science-fiction critic] Gary Wolfe, produce "the alienation of humanity from the very technological environments it has constructed in order to resolve its alienation from the universe".

It is difficult to comprehend the depth to which the atom bomb terrified the world, and America specifically, in the early cold war era. Richard Rhodes, author of the *The Making of the Atomic Bomb*, writes that "A nuclear weapon is in fact a total-death machine, compact and efficient" and quotes a Japanese study that concludes that the explosions at Hiroshima and Nagasaki were "the opening chapter to the annihilation of mankind." More than any single technological development, the atomic bomb made people think seriously about the end of the world. As a passport to Wolfe's icon of the wasteland, the bomb "teaches us that the unknown always remains, ready to reassert itself, to send us back to the beginning".

Bradbury first captures the general sense of anxiety felt in a new atomic age in the fifth chapter of *The Martian Chronicles*, "The Taxpayer." This short chapter identifies fear of nuclear war as an impetus for leaving Earth; the chapter also establishes itself as one of several in *Chronicles* that serve as precursors to *Fahrenheit 451* and centralize many of the early cold war themes Bradbury resumes in the second book: "There was going to be a big atomic war on Earth in about two years, and he didn't want to be here when it happened. He and thousands of others like him, if they had any sense, would go to Mars. See if they wouldn't! To get away from wars and censorship and statism and conscription and government control of this and that, of art and science!" . . .

Fahrenheit 451 resumes the examination of precarious existence in an atomic age that Bradbury began in *The Martian Chronicles.* Fire as the omnipotent weapon in *Fahrenheit* finds metaphoric parallels in the notion of the bomb as the omnipotent force in the cold war years. The early tests of the Los Alamos project, for example, paid close attention to the extreme temperatures produced by the fissioning and fusioning of critical elements. J. Robert Oppenheimer, Niels Bohr, and Edward Teller [physicists who created the first atomic bomb] based key decisions in the atomic bomb (and later the hydrogen bomb) designs on the core temperatures created at the moment of detonation. Montag and the Firemen of America, likewise, are ever conscious of the key numeral 451 (the temperature at which books burn), so much so that it is printed on their helmets. The linking of hubris with the attainment of power is evident in both the Los Alamos scientists and the Firemen as well.

As the Manhattan Project was drawing to a close, the team of physicists who designed the bomb came to exude a high degree of pride in their mastery of science, but without an attendant sense of responsibility. As Lamont explains, the bomb "represented the climax of an intriguing intellectual match between the scientists and the cosmos. The prospect of solving the bomb's cosmic mysteries, of having their calculations proved correct, seemed far more fascinating and important to the scientists than the prospect of their opening an era obsessed by fear and devoted to the control of those very mysteries". *Fahrenheit 451* opens with Montag similarly blinded by his own perceived importance: "He knew that when he returned to the firehouse, he might wink at himself, a minstrel man, burnt-corked [i.e., in blackface], in the mirror. Later, going to sleep, he would feel the fiery smile still gripped by his face muscles, in the dark. It never went away, that smile, it never ever went away, as long as he remembered". Like the engineers of atomic destruction, the engineer of intellectual destruction feels the successful completion of his goals entitles him to a legitimate smugness. The work of the cold war physicists, in retrospect, also shares something else with Montag, which Donald Watt points out: "Montag's destructive burning . . . is blackening, not enlightening; and it poses a threat to nature".

Fear of the Atomic World

Fahrenheit 451 also expands on the anxiety over the atomic bomb and fear of a nuclear apocalypse introduced in *Chronicles*. In *Fahrenheit*, Beatty endorses the official government position that, as "custodians of our peace of mind", he and Montag should "let [man] forget there is such a thing as war". Once Montag has decided to turn his back on the firehouse, however, he tries conveying his personal sense of outrage to Mildred at being kept ignorant, hoping to incite a similar concern in her: "How in hell did those bombers get up there every single second of our lives! Why doesn't someone want to talk about it! We've started and won two atomic wars since 1990!" Mildred, however, is perfectly uninspired and breaks off the conversation to wait for the White Clown to enter the TV screen. But Montag's unheeded warning becomes reality; the bombs are dropped once Montag meets up with Granger and the book people, . . . and Montag's horrific vision of the bomb's shock wave hitting the building where he imagines Mildred is staying captures a chilling image of his ignorant wife's last instant of life:

> Montag, falling flat, going down, saw or felt or imagined he saw or felt the walls go dark in Millie's face, heard her screaming, because in the millionth part of time left, she saw her own face reflected there, in a mirror instead of a

crystal ball, and it was such a wild empty face, all by itself in the room, touching nothing, starved and eating of itself, that at last she recognized it as her own and looked quickly up at the ceiling as it and the entire structure of the hotel blasted down upon her, carrying her with a million pounds of brick, metal, plaster, and wood, to meet other people in the hives below, all on their quick way down to the cellar where the explosion rid itself of them in its own unreasonable way.

Perhaps Bradbury's own sense of fear at a future that must accommodate atomic weapons had intensified between *The Martian Chronicles*'s publication in 1950 and *Fahrenheit 451*'s completion in 1953; perhaps what David Mogen identifies as Bradbury's inspiration for the book, Hitler's book burnings, affords little room for the comic. For whatever reasons, unlike *Chronicles*, which intersperses the solemnity of its nuclear aftermath chapters with a bit of lightness in the Walter Gripp story, *Fahrenheit* sustains a serious tone to the end of the book, even in its resurrectionist optimism for the future of the arts.

Optimism for the Future

This optimism for the future—this notion of recivilization—is the third common element between *The Martian Chronicles* and *Fahrenheit 451* that has early cold war connections. Given such nihilistic phenomena of the cold war era as its tendencies toward censorship, its socially paranoid outlook, and its budding arms race, it may seem a strange period to give rise to any optimism. However, one of the great ironies of the period was a peripheral belief that somehow the presence of nuclear arms would, by their very capacity to bring about ultimate destruction to all humans, engender a very special sort of cautiousness and cooperative spirit in the world heretofore not experienced. Perhaps there was a belief that Hiroshima and Nagasaki had taught us a big enough lesson in themselves about nuclear cataclysm that we as humans would rise above our destructive tendencies and live more harmoniously.

One very prominent figure who espoused this position was Dr. J. Robert Oppenheimer, the very man who headed the Los Alamos Manhattan Project. Oppenheimer would emerge as one of the most morally intriguing characters of the cold war. He was among the first in the scientific community to encourage restraint, caution, and careful deliberation in all matters regarding the pursuit of atomic energy. "There is only one future of atomic explosives that I can regard with any enthusiasm: that they should never be used in war," he said in a 1946 address before the George Westinghouse Centennial Forum. He also refused to participate in the development of the hydrogen bomb following Los Alamos, calling such a weapon "the plague of Thebes" [referring to the ancient Greek play *Oedipus the King*, in which the city of Thebes is suffering a terrible plague because of immorality]. In one of his most inspired addresses on the cooperation of art and science, Oppenheimer stated that "Both the man of science and the man of art live always at the edge of mystery, surrounded by it; both always, as the measure of their creation, have had to do with the harmonization of what is new with what is familiar, with the balance between novelty and synthesis, with the struggle to make partial order in total chaos. They can, in their work and in their lives, help themselves, help one another, and help all men". . . .

Bradbury's optimism for a recivilized world is also evident in the conclusion of *Fahrenheit 451*. The seed for an optimistic ending to this dystopian work is actually planted just before the bombs strike. As Montag makes his way across the wilderness, dodging the pursuit of the mechanical hound and the helicopters, he spots the campfire of the book people. His thoughts reflect an epiphany of his transformation from a destroyer of civilization to a builder of it: "[The fire] was not burning. It was warming. He saw many hands held to its warmth, hands without arms, hidden in darkness. Above the hands, motionless faces that were only moved and tossed and flickered with firelight. He hadn't known fire could look this way. He had never thought in his life that it could give as well as take".

This spirit of giving, of creating from the environment, is emphasized throughout the speeches given by Granger, the leader of the book preservers. In his allusion to the phoenix, which resurrects itself from the ashes of its own pyre, Granger's words reflect the new Montag, who can now see the life-sustaining properties of fire as well as its destructive powers; hopefully, Granger's words also contain hope for the American response to Hiroshima and Nagasaki: "we've got one damn thing the phoenix never had. We know the damn silly thing we just did. We know all the damn silly things we've done for a thousand years and as long as we know that and always have it around where we can see it, someday we'll stop making the goddamn funeral pyres and jumping in the middle of them". The book ends with Montag rehearsing in his mind a passage from the *Book of Revelation*, which he says he'll save for the reading at noon. [Literary critic] Peter Sisario sees in this ending "a key to Bradbury's hope that 'the healing of nations' can best come about through a rebirth of man's intellect"; Sisario's interpretation of *Fahrenheit*'s ending and Oppenheimer's interpretation of mankind's necessary response to the cold war share a belief in the triumph of the benevolent side of humans.

Peace and Aggression

A fourth theme in Bradbury's cold war novels that has a historical "objective correlative" is the dichotomous [divided] nature of the Cold War Man. The Cold War Man is a man antagonized by conflicting allegiances—one to his government, the other to his personal sense of morals and values—who is forced by circumstances to make an ultimate choice between these impulses. This Bradbury character type has roots in cold war political tensions.

During the early cold war years, the United States's international stance frequently wavered between a policy of military supremacy and one of peacetime concessions. . . .

These contradictory stances of peace and aggression in our nation's outlook occasionally found expression in the form of a single man during the early cold war. The figure of Dr. J. Robert Oppenheimer again becomes relevant. Though primarily remembered for his contribution to physics, Oppenheimer also had strong leanings toward the humanities; as a youth and in his years as a Harvard undergraduate, he developed a range of literary interests from the Greek classicists to [English poet John] Donne to [medieval Iranian writer] Omar Khayyam. David Halberstam observes, "To some he seemed the divided man—part creator of the most dangerous weapon in history—part the romantic innocent searching for some inner spiritual truth". For a government-employed physicist, however, this "division" would turn out to be something of a tragic flaw in the cold war years. When Oppenheimer would have no part of the U.S. government's decision to pursue the hydrogen bomb in its initial phase of the arms race with the Soviets, the government began an inquiry into his past. It was "determined" in June of 1954 that Oppenheimer was guilty of Communist associations that jeopardized national security. He was then stripped of his government security clearance, and his service with the Atomic Energy Commission terminated. Thus, in Oppenheimer was a man whose pacifistic sympathies eventually triumphed over his capacity for aggression—and in the early cold war years he was punished for it. . . .

The Divided Self

The dichotomous Cold War Man theme is again treated in *Fahrenheit 451*. Both Montag and Beatty are simultaneously capable of the destructive and appreciative of the artistic. As Donald Watt remarks of Montag, "Burning as constructive energy, and burning as apocalyptic catastrophe, are the symbolic poles of Bradbury's novel". Montag's divided self is clearly displayed by Bradbury at moments when his character is being influenced by the intellectually stimulating presences of Clarisse and Faber. Early in the book, when Montag is just beginning to wrestle with his identity as a fireman, Clarisse tells him that being a fireman "just doesn't seem right for you, somehow". Immediately Bradbury tells us that Montag "felt his body divide itself into a hotness and a coldness, a softness and a hardness, a trembling and a not trembling, the two halves grinding one upon the other".

Later, after offering his services to Faber and his group, Montag considers the shiftings of his own character that he has been feeling in his conflicting allegiances: "Now he knew that he was two people, that he was, above all, Montag, who knew nothing, who did not even know himself a fool, but only suspected it. And he knew that he was also the old man who talked to him and talked to him as the train was sucked from one end of the night city to the other". Fire Chief Beatty also suggests aspects of the Cold War Man. In spite of his wearing the role of the Official State Majority Leader as the fire chief and relentlessly burning every book at every alarm, Beatty acknowledges that he knows the history of Nicholas Ridley, the man burned at the stake alluded to by the woman who ignites her own home. He gives Montag the reply that most fire captains are "full of bits and pieces", however, when he later warns Montag against succumbing to the "itch" to read that every fireman gets "at least once in his career," he further adds an ambiguous disclosure: "Oh, to scratch that itch, eh? Well, Montag, take my word for it, I've had to read a few in my time to know what I was about, and the books say nothing! Nothing you can teach or believe". Though Beatty has an alibi for having some knowledge of literature, Bradbury urges us to question just what Beatty may not be telling us. Montag's later certainty over Beatty's desire to die at Montag's hands raises even more questions about Beatty's commitment to the destructive half of his duality.

Through *The Martian Chronicles* and *Fahrenheit 451*, Ray Bradbury has created a microcosm of early cold war tensions. Though the reader will perceive a degree of Bradbury's socio-political concerns from a reading of either novel, it is only through the reading of both as companion pieces that his full cold war vision emerges. From the perspective that America has wrestled itself free of the extremism of the McCarthyists and, thus far, has escaped nuclear war as well, Bradbury's cold war novels may have indeed contributed to the "prevention" of futures with cold war trappings.

Access to Books Is Important

Charles P. Hamblen

Charles P. Hamblen was an English teacher and principal of the Norwich Free Academy in Connecticut.

In the following essay Hamblen shares his experience as an English teacher trying to keep his students' attention on the books they were reading. Hamblen's experience teaching Ray Bradbury's Fahrenheit 451 *was enormously successful, as students connected to Bradbury's condemnation of censorship and his satirical humor. In the end,* Fahrenheit 451 *reminded Hamblen's students why having access to books is important.*

The realm of science fiction has yet to receive from literary critics and English teachers the respect accorded more established genres. To praise a science fiction writer is usually to do so apologetically, much as one praises a good B-movie by saying, "Yes, it's good . . . for a B-movie."

H.G. Wells, Aldous Huxley, and George Orwell are, of course, three writers who have avoided this general opprobrium, not only because their writing is patently great, but because they succeed in presenting world views which, while futuristic and problematic, do have a chilling relevance for our own time.

Ray Bradbury, however, has been subject to the type of condescension to which I refer, and perhaps justifiably. Right away he's got two strikes against him: (1) he hasn't produced anything of importance, that I know of, outside the science fiction field, and (2) he has a name that one associates more with a teen-age dance show host than with a significant writer. But I feel that he is important in that he has succeeded once

Charles P. Hamblen, "*Fahrenheit 451* in the Classroom," *English Journal*, vol. 57, no. 6, September 1968, pp. 818–24. Reproduced by permission.

or twice in projecting the very type of hollow, brutalizing negative utopia (or "dystopia," to accommodate Richard Lederer of St. Paul's School in New Hampshire) for which Huxley and Orwell, in particular, have become famous. For this reason, I think he rates inclusion in the study of some English classes, specifically those composed of students generally categorized as "hard to motivate," but who, nonetheless, can appreciate theme as well as plot if properly guided.

Two years ago, I tried [Bradbury's novel] *The Martian Chronicles* with just such a class. It was a disappointment. I found that the students were bothered by the disjointed, highly episodic nature of the book and consequently had trouble perceiving the overall theme: man's penchant, whether intentional or unintentional, for destroying whatever is good and beautiful in its natural state.

Students Connect with *Fahrenheit 451*

However, last year [1967] with *Fahrenheit 451*, I struck pay dirt. Those students with minimal perception were manifestly content with a slick, well-told adventure yarn which came as a welcome relief from the strain of having muddled through [Charles] Dickens and [William Shakespeare's] *Julius Caesar*. The more alert students, on the other hand, readily understood and were eager to discuss (with a little prodding) the thought-provoking implications of the novel.

Fahrenheit 451 pictures an Orwellian society of the near future where Happiness is the end, conformity and continuous entertainment the means to that end. Original thought is outlawed; the possession of books is a crime against the state. Firemen, not policemen, are the principal guardians of law and order. Only these firemen don't put out fires; they start them wherever they find a hidden cache of books.

The students, I found, tended to identify with and root for Montag, a fireman who becomes disenchanted in turn with his job, his cretinous [unintelligent] wife (whose mind has long since turned to mush under the incessant pounding of state-controlled entertainment), and the anesthetized society of which she is a symptom. No one communicates with anyone else on any but the most superficial level because the senses are completely inundated by constant sound and music blaring from vast TV-walls and transistor radios. Students were here reminded of the throbbing cacophony of their own dances, in which each partner seems lost in a dazed world of his own as he sways to the hypnotic beat. They laughed at Bradbury's brilliantly satirical dialogue, particularly in those scenes where Montag tries to get through to his wife.

Oh, she walked to the bath again. "Did something happen [last night]?"

"A fire, is all."

"I had a nice evening," she said, in the bathroom.

"What doing?"

"The parlor."

"What was on?"

"Programs."

"What programs?"

"Some of the best ever."

"Who?"

"Oh, you know, the bunch."

"Yes the bunch, the bunch, the bunch." He pressed at the pain in his eyes and suddenly the odor of kerosene made him vomit.

Mildred came in humming. She was surprised. "Why'd you do that?"

He looked in dismay at the floor. "We burned an old woman with her books."

"It's a good thing the rug's washable." She fetched a mop and worked on it. . . .

The parlor was exploding with sound.

Why Books Are Important

The nucleus of the book, a section ready-made for clarifying the theme to students, is the scene in which Captain Beatty, Montag's ironically paternal superior, explains the evolution of their society to his wavering henchman. The change began with the invention of photography, Beatty asserts. This led to motion pictures, radio, and television. These media appealed to the masses; hence simplicity became of paramount importance. To parallel the rapid pace of twentieth-century life, books were condensed, first to digests, ultimately to dictionary resumés. Reflective thought was virtually eliminated. Entertainment, "super-super sports," and the immediate gratification of the senses held the populace in thrall. (It's interesting to note that Bradbury wrote *Fahrenheit 451* more than a decade before the evolution of "Super Sunday" [the first Super Bowl was played in 1967] and "The Now Generation [referring to the 1960s generation]." What books and magazines did survive were completely watered down to avoid the rancor of vociferous minorities. Automation completed the trek to total non-intellectuality. Censorship was almost an afterthought, merely established to stifle those few, stubborn, philosophical souls who occasionally cropped up.

As he finishes his bravura performance, Beatty sums up the fireman's position:

The important thing for you to remember, Montag, is we're The Happiness Boys, The Dixie Duo, you and I and the others. We stand against the small tide of those who want to make everyone unhappy with conflicting theory and thought. We have our fingers in the dike. Hold steady. Don't let the torrent of melancholy and drear philosophy drown our world. We depend on you. I don't think you realize how important *you* are, *we* are, to our happy world as it stands now.

This is Bradbury at his satirical, hard-hitting best and it effectively structured the students' thinking about the rest of the book. They could see why, in that terrible, antiseptic time, rocking chairs and front porches were abolished, why people talked but didn't *say* anything, why the human soul atrophied, and why Beatty indirectly committed suicide. And most significantly, they saw why books are important.

Now, if they'll only remember.

Mock Book Burning Elicits Strong Feelings

Robert Gardner

Robert Gardner is a language arts teacher at Apollo High School in St. Cloud, Minnesota.

In this selection Gardner discusses one of the most radical lessons he has ever taught in the classroom. To bring to life the topic of Ray Bradbury's Fahrenheit 451, *Gardner brought his students to the science lab and, together, they burned books. Student reaction was mixed, ranging from outrage to excitement over firing up pages. The most significant lesson they learned, thought Gardner, was that when people get caught up in a situation, they easily abandon their sensible impulses.*

I have burned a book. Several, actually. And it was a pleasure to burn. I was searching for a way to introduce Ray Bradbury's *Fahrenheit 451* to my Science Fiction classes. The day before we started the novel, I had the idea to see if a science lab was available when I had class. Could we experiment to discover the temperature at which paper burns? Schedules meshed, and I began to look for books to burn.

Why books? Obviously, since Bradbury focuses on burning books, I naturally locked in on finding books to burn. It seemed the appropriate thing to do. But I could have just used blank sheets of paper or old newspapers. What significance does a language arts [LA] teacher burning a book have—even if tied to a lesson?

The Book Burning

The first hour we tried the experiment, it did not work well. Yes, the book burned. It blazed. But to catch the temperature

Robert Gardner, "A New Fashioned Book Burning," *The English Journal*, vol. 86, no. 2, February 1997. Copyright © 1997 by the National Council of Teachers of English. Reprinted with permission.

at which paper begins to burn is difficult—a sophisticated act—for once it starts to burn, the temperature quickly soars past the point of ignition. Our thermometer topped out at 360 degrees Celsius—much more than 600 degrees Fahrenheit. Afterward the students and I discussed the reasons people would want to burn books, and the feeling of the not-quite-successful experiment lingered over the class.

A couple of periods later, as students entered for my next section of Science Fiction, they were anxious. They wanted to know if we would burn a book. No, that's not entirely true—they didn't want to know, they wanted to burn.

We raced to the science lab, and an electricity filled the room. But first we had a spirited, frenzied discussion. Why were they excited? It's fun to burn, they said. Why, I wanted to know. There's an adrenaline rush. But more than that, there's control. There's a risk—burning is often illegal; it is a forbidden act. The students know (or at least believe) that it is wrong to burn, so for many it becomes a forbidden-fruit temptation. Control of nature.

As I readied for the final burn, two students whom I knew but who were not in Science Fiction accosted me in the hallway. "Who are you to pass judgment on those books? What you are doing is wrong. We have lost respect for you because you are burning books." They lacked the context of the class discussion, but apparently the experiment—now more a social than scientific one—already was reverberating throughout the school. (Later I was able to calm them down by explaining these were, truthfully, damaged books that were to be thrown away.)

Students' Reactions

I return to my earlier question: what significance does a language arts teacher burning a book have—even if tied to a lesson? I put the question to my students, asking for their reac-

Members of the Nazi Youth participated in burning Jewish-Marxist books in 1938 Nazi Germany. High school teacher Robert Gardner believes the thrill of something can overpower a person's sensible impulses. AP Images.

tion to my actions. While most understood the intended point of the lesson, not all agreed with what I did:

- "It is somewhat ironic for a language arts teacher to burn a book because this is what they believe in and enjoy—literature."

- "People burn books for all kinds of reasons. What the reason for doing it is really doesn't matter. It is the idea of ruining all of the work in research and knowledge that the book they are burning contains. So in short, no, I don't think it was right for Mr. Gardner to burn that book."

- "In the mind of most high school students, the idea of an LA teacher burning a book is off the wall. I can see him doing it to draw the attention of the students and to get his point across, but I still disagree with it."

- "In this particular case it wasn't wrong for Mr. Gardner to burn the book. This was only a demonstration for a class. He didn't do it out of hatred."
- "I don't think it's one of those things you should do in front of a crowd to entertain."
- "No, I don't agree that he should have burned that book. I think by explaining it, that it was good enough. I feel that it was kind of a waste by him doing that."
- "You are supposed to show respect for what you teach about."
- "That book represents our freedom to write, read, and think whatever we want to. Society's in trouble. If LA teachers, those people who are to advocate, and teach people to understand books, start burning them, we're all in big trouble."
- "It was cool when Gardner burned the book, but it wasn't right. He was destroying someone's freedom of speech, expression, and their ideas. He didn't need to burn it; he could have just told us what we are going to read. Most language arts teachers don't burn books because reading is one thing they try to get us to do. Most teachers don't demonstrate the book, they just tell you to read this by a certain date."

What did the students—and I—learn? Fire is a more powerful tool than I imagined. Students wanted to burn books; they wanted the thrill of doing the forbidden, the scandalous. I learned a lesson I did not start out to teach: that getting caught up in the action, in the thrill of something can overrule our more sensible impulses. This, of course, is one of Bradbury's points as well.

Will I burn books again? Probably, but I will do so with the knowledge that students' immediate reaction to flames curling books' pages proves that *Fahrenheit 451* is closer to fact than I'd like.

Consumerism Makes Conformity Easy

David Seed

David Seed is a professor of English at Liverpool University in England and the author of Imagining Apocalypse: Studies in Cultural Crisis.

In this essay Seed argues that society's extreme consumerism in Ray Bradbury's Fahrenheit 451 *wipes out political awareness, individuality, and personal ownership. In the book, political references focus on mere names and appearances; individuals are viewed only as consumers, and people have no sense of personal ownership, not even of their homes. In order to cope with this erasure of self and the constant destructive noise of the television, sleeping pills become part of the political institution. Seed contends that to reveal the totalitarianism of this state, Bradbury uses the dissatisfaction of a single individual, Montag.*

[In] Ray Bradbury's *Fahrenheit 451* (1953) [not] only is the protagonist Montag initially a robot too, he is also a member of the state apparatus which enforces such prescriptions [of conformity] by destroying the books which might counteract the solicitations of the media. The regime of the novel masks its totalitarianism with a facade of material prosperity. Montag's superior Beatty explains its coming-into-being as a benign process of inevitable development, everything being justified on the utilitarian grounds of the majority's happiness: "technology, mass exploitation, and minority pressure carried the trick, thank God." A levelling-down is presented as a triumph of technological know-how and of

David Seed, "The Flight from the Good Life: 'Fahrenheit 451' in the Context of Postwar American Dystopias," *Journal of American Studies*, vol. 28, no. 2, 1994. Copyright © 1994 by Cambridge University Press. Reprinted with the permission of Cambridge University Press.

system; above all it was a spontaneous transformation of society not a dictatorial imposition ("it didn't come from the Government down"). Bradbury's description of the media draws on [Aldous Huxley's] *Brave New World* as confirmed by postwar developments in television. Observing the latter boom in America, Huxley commented: "In *Brave New World* nonstop distractions of the most fascinating nature . . . are deliberately used as instruments of policy, for the purpose of preventing people from paying too much attention to the realities of the social and political situation." He continues in terms directly relevant to the world of Bradbury's novel: "A society, most of whose members spend a great deal of their time . . . in the irrelevant other worlds of sport and soap opera . . . will find it hard to resist the encroachments of those who would manipulate and control it." Where Beatty minimizes the firemen's role as benevolent guardians of the status quo, Huxley refuses such a tendentiously spontaneous account in order to pinpoint political purpose.

The result of this process in *Fahrenheit 451* is a consumer culture completely divorced from political awareness. An aural refrain running through the novel is the din of passing bombers which has simply become background noise. This suggests a total separation of political action from everyday social life and correspondingly when Montag's wife Millie and her friends agree to "talk politics" the discussion revolves entirely around the names and appearances of the figures concerned. In other words the latter have become images within a culture dominated by television. "The Fireman" (the first version of *Fahrenheit 451*) summarizes the typical programmes as follows:

> . . . there on the screen was a man selling orange soda pop and a woman drinking it with a smile; how could she drink and smile simultaneously? A real stunt! Following this, a demonstration of how to bake a certain new cake, followed by a rather dreary domestic comedy, a news analysis that

did not analyze anything and did not mention the war, even though the house was shaking constantly with the flight of new jets from four directions, and an intolerable quiz show naming state capitals.

The very tempo of this list, a rapid sequence of short items, has been explained by Beatty as economy ("the centrifuge flings off all unnecessary, time-wasting thought") but the discourse of production has now become contradictory as it has been displaced onto consumption. If commercial efficiency notionally releases workers to enjoy new leisure opportunities, the aim of the new media is to fill that leisure time not to economize on it.

The Dehumanizing Effects of the Media

The novel significantly magnifies the references to TV which occur in "The Fireman" on to a larger scale. Montag's living room has become a 3-D televisual environment for his wife who dreams of adding a fourth wall-screen so that the house will seem no longer theirs but "exotic people's." One of Montag's earliest realizations in the novel is that his house is exactly like thousands of others. Identical and therefore capable of substitution, it can never be his own. That is why the clichéd designation by the media of Millie as "homemaker" is so absurdly ironic because at the very moment when the television is promoting one role it is also feeding her with desires which push in the opposite direction, ultimately inviting her to identify with another place preferable to her more mundane present house. *Fahrenheit 451* dramatizes the effects of the media as substitutions. Millie finds an ersatz intimacy with the "family" on the screen which contrasts markedly with her relation to Montag. Again and again the dark space of their bedroom is stressed, its coldness and silence; whereas Millie's favourite soap operas keep up a constant hubbub and medley of bright colours.

Millie and her friends are defined entirely by their roles as consumers, whether of sedatives, soap-operas, or fast cars. Bradbury anticipates [Canadian social scientist] Marshall McLuhan by presenting the media which stimulate this consumption as extensions of faculties (the thimble anticipations of Walkmans) or their substitutes (the toaster has hands to save her the trouble of touching the bread). A bizarre passage Bradbury planned to include in the novel pushes the dehumanizing effects of the media to Gothic extremes:

> They sat in the room with the little electronic vampires feeding silently at their throats, touching at their jugulars with great secretness. Their faces were masked over with black velvet, and their bodies were draped in such a way as not to prove whether man or woman sat there beneath. And the hands were gloved with thickened, sexless material; and only the faintest gleam showed in the slits of their eyes, in the half dark twilight room.

Here dress performs a near total erasure of feature and even gender, replacing skin with an insulating patina. Bradbury's application of the vampire myth stresses loss of vitality whereas Marshall McLuhan draws on the story of Narcissus: "This extension of himself by mirror numbed his perceptions until he became the servomechanism of his own extended or repeated image." The result in both cases is immobility and the creation of a closed system between the individual and technology which, in the Bradbury passage quoted above, drains off the sociability of the gathering described. Mildred's house combines all the electronic gadgetry associated with the fifties "good life."

A Willing Flight

But these things have a cost. Bradbury further anticipates McLuhan in rendering television as an aggressive medium: "Music bombarded him at such an immense volume that his bones were almost shaken from his tendons," and then, as it quietens down, "you had the impression that someone had turned on a washing-machine or sucked you up in a gigantic vacuum." The experience of one consumable can only be understood through comparison with another, and here the individual is put into a posture of maximum passivity as subjected to machines, not their controller. McLuhan explains the television in far more positive terms, but still ones which partly echo Bradbury's. Thus "with TV, the viewer is the screen. He is bombarded with light impulses." And because TV is no good for background it makes more demands on the viewer than does radio: "Because the low definition of TV insures a high degree of audience involvement, the most effective programs are those that present situations which consist of some process to be completed." Bradbury burlesques this notion of audience participation as no more than an electronic trick whereby an individual's name can be inserted into a gap in the announcer's script (and even his lip-movements adjusted).

The media in Bradbury's novel then induce a kind of narcosis [unconsciousness induced by a narcotic drug]. There is both a continuity and an analogy between Millie watching the wall-screens and then taking sleeping pills. Similarly in *Brave New World* the opiate soma has become the religion of the people. Huxley subsequently explained that "the soma habit was not a private vice; it was a political institution." . . .

Questioning Consumerism

[In other stories, the impetus of the plot carries characters away from their culture.] The essential trigger to that flight is supplied by an alienation not only from suburban monotony but also from Montag's consumer-wife. He contemplates her as if she has ceased to be a human being: ". . . he saw her without opening his eyes, her hair burnt by chemicals to a brittle straw, her eyes with a kind of cataract unseen but suspect far behind the pupils, the reddened pouting lips, the body as thin as a praying mantis from dieting, and her flesh like white bacon." Millie here fragments into disparate features transformed by dye, cosmetics or dieting. Instead of being the consumer she is now consumed by commercially induced processes. The passage points backwards to an original state which is no longer recoverable and in that respect the images approach the free-floating state of simulation described by [French sociologist] Jean Baudrillard. In the contemporary phase of capitalism, he argues, abstraction and simulation now involve the "generation by models of a real without origin or reality: a hyperreal." Signs now become substitutions for the real, at their most extreme bearing no relation to any reality. It is the penultimate phase of the image or sign, however, which best glosses Bradbury's novel, namely when the image "masks the *absence* of a basic reality". The adjective "reddened" only appears to suggest a physical state prior to make-up. Later in the novel when Millie flees from the house without lipstick her mouth is simply "gone," as if the adjective has grotesquely taken over actuality from its referent.

Montag clearly functions as a satirical means for Bradbury to question the impetus of consumerism and passages like the one just quoted estrange Montag from an environment he has been taking for granted. [American science- fiction writer] Frederik Pohl likewise exploits estrangement effects in "The Tunnel under the World" (1954). . . .

Where Pohl briefly surveys the control of a whole environment Bradbury sets up contrasts between different kinds of social space in *Fahrenheit 451*, particularly between interiors and exteriors. A 1951 short story, "The Pedestrian," anticipates these themes and describes a point of transition just before the uniformity of the novel is finally established. The subject is simple: a pedestrian is arrested for walking the streets at night. The opening paragraph introduces an iterative account of what the protagonist has been doing for ten years:

To enter out into that silence that was the city at eight o'clock of a misty evening in November, to put your feet upon that buckling concrete walk, step over grassy seams and make your way, hands in pockets, through the silences, that was what Mr. Leonard Mead most dearly loved to do. He would stand upon the corner of an intersection and peer down long moonlit avenues of sidewalk in four directions, deciding which way to go, but it really made no difference; he was alone in this world of 2053 A.D. . . .

Acts of Resistance

Bradbury's infinitives and then his use of the hypothetical second person draw the reader into a pattern of action which turns out to be a rhetorical cul-de-sac because Mead, it transpires, is the last of his line pursuing a habit which has become obsolete. The unusual opening phrase destabilizes our distinction between interior and exterior space and the description then draws on post-romantic survival narratives like Mary Shelley's *The Last Man* to suggest an ultimate state of isolation. But Mead stands in ironic proximity to a new species of citizens who, in anticipation of Millie, fill their leisure time watching television. Even the police car which arrests Mead (since there are no officers inside it is literally the car which does the arresting) is the last of its line since there is no longer any urban crime, and the story concludes with Mead being taken away to the "Psychiatric Center for Research On Regressive Tendencies," thereby signalling the demise of a social possibility. When Bradbury worked this story into his novel it became part of the regime's past, helping to explain why in *Fahrenheit 451* the nocturnal streets are either deserted or used as improvised race tracks.

It is of course a truism that the dystopias of the fifties base themselves on the premise that dissatisfaction with the prevalent regime will be registered sooner or later by their protagonists. In order to accelerate this process of realization some novelists use catalyst-figures whose role is to function as a productive irritant in the protagonist's consciousness. So Clarisse, the niece it turns out of Leonard Mead, fascinates and disturbs Montag because she seems wilfully to stand outside social norms. Neither child nor woman, she introduces herself as a social misfit ("I'm seventeen and I'm crazy") and challenges Montag to confront awkward questions such as whether he is happy. . . .

Fahrenheit 451 and [Kurt Vonnegut's novel] *Player Piano* both narrate a dual process of learning and disengagement where the protagonist's field of consciousness supplies the ground of the action, indeed even becomes the central issue within that action. At one point Clarisse declares "this is the age of the disposable tissue," a strategic pun on Bradbury's part which relates directly to Vonnegut's novel also since both writers are describing acts of resistance towards social and economic systems where human beings have become dispensable material. Characters accordingly are grouped oppositionally around the protagonists. . . .

Dissatisfaction of One Individual Reveals Totalitarianism

In *Fahrenheit 451* Clarisse and then later an English professor named Faber stimulate Montag towards overt resistance, whereas Beatty functions as antagonist. From a very early stage in the novel Montag internalizes Beatty's voice as a censorious or punitive force, the voice of the superego [Sigmund Freud's psychic factor representing internalized social norms] resisting taboo thoughts or actions. Every scene where Beatty figures then becomes charged with ambiguity as if he is accusing Montag of crimes. When the latter comes down with a "fever" Beatty visits him without being called, explaining that he could foresee what was going to happen. In a simulation of a doctor's visit Beatty tries to deindividualize Montag's problem as a typical case which will pass. If we visualize Montag being addressed on the one side by Beatty and on the other by

Faber like a morality play, although the latter occupies the moral high ground, Beatty represents a far more sinister presence by his uncanny knack of predicting what Montag will think. [Director of the film version of *Fahrenheit 451*] Francois Truffaut described the action as "une forme de lutte contre l'autorité" [a form of struggle against authority] and Montag must kill Beatty as the personification of that authority however euphemistically the latter presents his power.

The key progression in this process is a shift from the latent to the overt, from the implicit to the explicit. Montag discovers an inner voice which he has been suppressing and his previously unified self fractures into dissociations of mind from body and limb from limb: "His hands had been infected, and soon it would be his arms. He could feel the poison work up his wrists and into his elbows and his shoulders, and then the hump-over from shoulder-blade to shoulder-blade like a spark leaping a gap. His hands were ravenous. And his eyes were beginning to feel hunger. . . ." The metaphor of poison encodes Montag's dissidence within the ideology of a regime devoted to maintaining the so-called health of the body politic; but the displaced hunger of his other limbs suggests a desire that will take him out of that dominant ideology. We can see from this passage how the issue of authority pervades the very style of the novel.

In his 1968 article "Death Warmed Over" Bradbury mounts a spirited defence of classic horror movies and fantasy fiction by contrasting two broad artistic methods: the accumulation of fact and the use of symbolism. He condemns the former as being appropriate to another discipline altogether: "We have fallen into the hands of the scientists, the reality people, the data collectors." And he goes on to propose selective resonance as an alternative. "The symbolic acts, not the minuscule details of the act, are everything." Retrospectively this article helps to explain the method of *Fahrenheit 451* which, like the other dystopias of the period, uses the dissatisfaction of one individual to reflect on the general inadequacies of a regime perceived as in some sense totalitarian.

A Mistake in *Fahrenheit 451* Echoes Bradbury's Themes

Joseph F. Brown

Joseph F. Brown was affiliated with Louisiana State University when he wrote this article for the journal the Explicator.

In Ray Bradbury's Fahrenheit 451, *when Captain Beatty explains to Fireman Montag why it is necessary for all members of society to be alike, he claims to quote from the Constitution of the United States. But there is an error here: the quotation Beatty uses is from the Declaration of Independence, not the Constitution. In this viewpoint, Brown discusses the implications of this error, hypothesizing whether it was Beatty's or Bradbury's. According to Brown, if it was Bradbury's error, it would seem to contradict the author's argument against the inattentiveness to literature he condemns in his book.*

In an important scene in Ray Bradbury's novella *Fahrenheit 451*, Captain Beatty (the leader of the firemen tasked with burning books in a futuristic, dystopian society) articulates for Montag (the protagonist) the fundamental idea underpinning the laws and norms of this oppressive and ignorant society. "We must all be alike," explains Beatty, "not everyone born free and equal, as the Constitution says, but everyone made equal". Of course, this is a mistake. The phrase to which Beatty refers is found in the Declaration of Independence (1776), not the Constitution of the United States (1788). This is no small matter; separated by more than a decade, these documents had different purposes and audiences. Beatty's (or Bradbury's) confusion is significant when seen in the context of the work's larger concern over the loss of literacy (and, ul-

Joseph F. Brown, "As the Constitution Says: Distinguishing Documents in Ray Bradbury's *Fahrenheit 451*," *The Explicator*, vol. 67, Fall 2008. Copyright © 2008. Reproduced by permission of Taylor & Francis Group, LLC.

timately, knowledge) in modern society. But is the mistake the character's or the author's? The implications of each possibility open up levels of understanding this novella and its place in contemporary American culture.

A Remarkable Error

If the error is Beatty's, it is important because it is precisely the kind of mistake a citizen of *Fahrenheit 451*'s dystopian society would make. Beatty is, after all, a product of his culture and, as readers later learn, a staunch advocate of its fundamental ideas. The novella presents a future in which reading has been cast aside by a society that prefers wall-sized televisions and "sea-shell" portable radios. In response, the government provides "firemen" to burn the remaining books in accordance with society's will. Bradbury frequently emphasizes that the law banning books descended from such a preference. As a result, society has become vapid, more interested in mindless entertainment than knowledge, understanding, and critical thought, and the ability to discern between two fundamental documents has no place.

If intentional, Bradbury has packaged the mistaking of the Declaration of Independence for the Constitution along with a notable corruption of the famous line to which Beatty refers. That line, taught in elementary schools across the country each year, comes from the Declaration's second paragraph: "We hold these Truths to be self-evident, that all Men are created equal, that they are endowed by their Creator with certain unalienable Rights, that among these are Life, Liberty, and the Pursuit of Happiness." The difference between these two concepts, "created equal" and "made equal," is precisely what Bradbury's novella is about: the power of language and the tyranny of its misuse, censorship, or absence. In his speech, Beatty describes a society moved to self-censorship at the behest of minority interests to the point that, eventually, all literature is deemed offensive. People should not have to feel ig-

Guy Montag (Oskar Werner) stands with Clarisse (Julie Christie), in a scene from the film Fahrenheit 451. © John Springer Collection/Corbis.

norant or inferior to others, Beatty suggests, and such censorship is done to provide and ensure happiness. He explains, "Each man the image of every other; then all are happy, for there are no mountains to make them cower, to judge themselves against". Yet, in its effort to provide such happiness, in making it, the culture ironically denies it. After all, Bradbury suggests, a culture without literature lacks the imagination and perhaps even the language needed to articulate its possibilities for happiness. It is significant, then, that Beatty has mistaken the document steeped in such revolutionary energy (and dedicated to imagining and articulating the principles of a new society previously stultified by oppression) for the document whose aim, more than ten years later, was to articulate the organs and mechanisms by which such a government would deliver that freedom. The mistake is remarkable both because Beatty is the product of a fictional society that has failed so miserably to do so, and because Bradbury, in his jeremiac lament [expressing a bitter lament or righteous prophecy of doom characteristic of the Old Testament prophet Jeremiah], wished to warn readers against cultural changes that he feared would lead to ruin.

If the Error Were Bradbury's

On the other hand, Bradbury makes a point of showing his readers that Beatty is not just a regular product of his society. He is, after all, unlike its most representative citizen: Montag's wife, Mildred. By the end of the work, she has betrayed Montag to Beatty, attempted suicide (only to forget—or pretend to forget—that she tried), and otherwise shown herself to be a selfish, vacuous, childish person. She is so devoid of introspection and reflection that, at one point, Montag discovers that she cannot even remember how they met. By contrast, Beatty appears to have been educated. He has, Montag learns, read a great deal of books, even if his experience with them led him to become a staunch supporter of book burning. In fact, he is the only character posited as an intellectual counter to Faber, the ex-professor who provides Montag with guidance and knowledge. This is evident in the climactic scene of the second part, "The Sieve and the Sand," in which Beatty and Montag (with Faber vicariously present through Montag's hidden earpiece) debate, essentially, the value of knowledge. Beatty does not debate Montag so much as himself (playing devil's advocate to his own arguments to illustrate, he thinks, the contradictory nature of textual knowledge). In other words, if Beatty can recite from memory Alexander Pope's "Essay on Criticism" or Samuel Johnson's *Rasselas,* is it reasonable to believe that he would confuse two of the most important, fundamental documents in the American tradition?

This leaves the possibility that the error lies with Bradbury. Confusing the source of this iconic phrase is, unfortunately, exceedingly easy to do. One possibility is that both the Declaration of Independence and the Constitution have achieved a kind of platitudinous status and, therefore, many Americans seem to feel that they know these documents by virtue of "living" them. In another, more frightening possibility, this confusion signals a slippage in the power of language and the written word in contemporary culture not unlike the slippage depicted in *Fahrenheit 451.* In this ironic scenario, Bradbury is guilty of the same inattention that his book argues breeds ignorance.

Like many communities across the country in 2008, Baton Rouge [Louisiana] participated in the National Endowment for the Arts's [NEA] "Big Read" program by reading *Fahrenheit 451.* The book was, no doubt, a popular choice for many participating in the program due in large part to concerns over the state of literacy in America. For example, a recent study conducted by the NEA, "To Read or Not to Read," found that Americans are spending less time reading and that, as a result, reading-comprehension skills are drastically eroding. If Bradbury's novella is to be posited and lauded in libraries and classrooms across the country as the great shield against a slide into illiteracy and ignorance, it is fitting to submit its basic tenets to the same scrutiny and close reading that it suggests are the bedrock of social and civic responsibility.

Fahrenheit 451 Comes Close to Describing the Future

David T. Wright

David T. Wright is a regular contributor to the alternative print and online journal the Last Ditch.

In this article Wright argues that of all futuristic stories, Ray Bradbury's Fahrenheit 451 *comes closest to the present reality. Published in 1953, Bradbury's book is an eerily prophetic description of the dangers of the "information society." For example, Bradbury predicted the constant presence of television in homes, something most could not have imagined when Bradbury was writing his novel. In a twist of irony, Bradbury's book about censorship eventually became itself the victim of censorship.*

Remember how the future used to be? Great clean cities with robot-controlled cars zooming safely along graceful, broad freeways. Homes in which every task was done by machine, every need seen to with the help of advanced technology. A helicopter in every garage. Supersonic family excursions to Antarctica. Little Johnny riding his levitation scooter to visit Great Grandma, who was 120 but looked 55. Clean, safe, and abundant nuclear power. Prosperous colonies on Mars. You get the picture.

That's how the future looked when I was a kid. Magazines such as *Popular Mechanics* had articles about cars that would turn into airplanes, the automated Kitchen of the Future, hovercraft ocean liners, and telephones with little video screens in them. And as Man became more technologically advanced, it was just assumed that he would also become more advanced socially. He would learn how to be nice instead of envious,

David T. Wright, "The Incendiary Prophet," *The Last Ditch*, August 1995. Copyright © 1995 by Thornwalker.com. Reproduced by permission.

lustful, greedy, slothful, gluttonous, jealous, and hateful. So, naturally, there would be no more poverty, no more war, no more crime—or at least much less of such previously universal afflictions. We would all become one big, happy, albeit disgustingly homogenized, family.

The New Future

How things have changed. Today [in 1995], the popular vision is exactly opposite. Expressed in novels, television, and movies, life in today's future is like [English philosopher Thomas] Hobbes's state of nature—or the future posited by Nicholas Strakon in [his essay] *Dark Suits and Red Guards*: solitary, poor, nasty, brutish, and short. In George Lucas's 1971 movie "THX-1138," for instance, the Suits and Guards have achieved a high-tech, anthill-like society in which numbers have replaced names and sex is a crime—one shaven-headed Guard harpy rants maniacally against physical love the way ours do against tobacco, child abuse, or, well, normal physical love. In Arnold Schwarzenegger's exceedingly profitable "Terminator" movies, evil robots have taken over the world of the future and are trying to exterminate the human race. Other Ahnuld sci-fi movies have similarly pessimistic plots, for instance "The Running Man," in which individuals who offend the state are vicariously hunted to the death by contestants in a TV game show ("Ah'll be beck!" growls Ahnuld to the sleazy game show host. "Only in the reruns," is the gleeful reply). The syndicated TV show "Babylon 5" gives us a galaxy torn by war between different species, with an exhausted human race that has narrowly escaped being wiped out and is now tyrannized by a sort of mind-reading secret police called the "Psi-Corps."

The only major exception to this trend seems to be the popular "Star Trek" movies and TV series, '60s throwbacks that still envision a nauseatingly progressive future in which Man has "evolved" into a more enlightened and politically correct—not to mention deadly boring—entity. It's hard to decide which is worse, a future of chaos and collapse, or one Sanitized for Our Protection, devoid of any real passion or conflict, brightened only by the sight of the luscious, tightly clad Counselor Troi. Even here, though, humanity is supposed to have gone through a quasi-apocalyptic upheaval before achieving technocratic, psychotherapeutic nirvana.

The different apocalyptic scenarios seem to fall into two broad groups, usually containing elements of both. The lesser of the two is the environmental- or technological-disaster category, which includes worlds destroyed by nuclear war (Nevil Shute's novel *On the Beach*, the TV miniseries "The Day After," the film "The Road Warrior"), global warming or pollution (the film "Blade Runner"), overpopulation (the film "Soylent Green," James Blish's novel *A Torrent of Faces*), or the above-mentioned killer robots (the rather bad Australian film "Hardware").

The second, and more important category, is the *1984* [a novel by George Orwell] or *Brave New World* [a novel by Aldous Huxley] scenario, in which the state or big business has enslaved or is in the process of enslaving the human race. Passable examples of this tendency are "THX-1138," "The Running Man," "Blade Runner" (mega-corporation creates synthetic human slaves), "Soylent Green" (sheeple are encouraged to die so that their bodies can be fed to those who remain), "They Live" (a movie in which the human race is unknowingly enslaved by aliens with whom the upper classes collaborate), and "Logan's Run" (deracinated, decultured subjects lead shallow, hedonistic lives and are killed before they become old). In most instances, enslavement has brought with it increasing levels of domestic criminality and chaos; in some, the regime keeps a tight, orderly lid on things.

Is it a mistake to attach too much importance to this trend? After all, it's not hard to imagine why such scenarios are so popular in today's Land of the Free. It's a lot more difficult to throw in a lot of ultraviolence, spectacular flaming explosions, flying blood and body parts, the f-word, exposed sexual paraphernalia, and all the other uplifting staples of the modern Hollywood flick if your screenplay assumes a tranquil, perfect society. Surely, the Future as Dystopia tendency owes much of its strength to the ease with which a novelist or producer can get away with all kinds of gaudy, debauched backgrounds, bizarre costumes, and weird and violent behavior, without the constraints of consistency and realism imposed by contemporary or historical settings.

But having said that, I think it's obvious that such scenarios also strike a chord in our hearts. In each case they reflect some aspect of what is happening around us, not to mention to us. As we descend ever further into slavery and degradation, it becomes ever more natural just to accept, even if unconsciously, the idea that more of the same awaits us. I don't know exactly how, but I think this constitutes much of the appeal of such scenarios.

Polite Totalitarianism

None of my examples—not even George Orwell's *1984*—comes closer to describing our actual future than one of the granddaddies of the genre: Ray Bradbury's *Fahrenheit 451*. (Note: in deference to Mr. Bradbury, this review applies only to the new Ballantine/Del Rey paperback, for reasons that will become apparent later.) I first read it when I bought it through the Scholastic Book Club in sixth grade. (What delicious irony—remember when sixth-graders were expected to be able to read adult books?)

Unlike most of its successors, imitators, etc., Bradbury's novel—or novella, really—is an inspired criticism of what we now call the "information society," and the yawning chasm it is creating in our collective soul. In it he managed to predict with frightening accuracy such current social pathologies as the dumbing down of popular entertainment and education, our growing addiction to empty sensory stimulation, the rise of random violence among youth, the increasing anomie and alienation among everyone, the cult of pharmaciae, the cult of consumerism, the cult of the victim and the resulting right of everyone (except normal white people) never to be offended, our increasing atomization, and, neither last nor least, the assault on truth and the life of the mind, which of course includes our society's increasingly vicious attacks on Christianity. In short, Bradbury was able to discern the outlines of today's Polite Totalitarianism. The amazing thing is that he did it more than 40 years ago.

Bradbury's protagonist, Guy Montag, is a fireman. His job is to respond to alarms, like today's firemen (sorry, "firefighters," soon to be changed, no doubt, to "People Who Lead Firefighting Lives")—but not to put fires out. His sole duty is to burn books and the houses in which they are found. Thus the title: 451 degrees Fahrenheit is the temperature at which paper begins to burn. Montag and his colleagues start fires with a hose that squirts kerosene. I remember that the book itself seemed to smell of kerosene. Probably that was just owing to the solvents in the ink; but it added to the story's considerable impact on my soft, impressionable young mind.

Montag's world is a gilded cage of physical luxury and total spiritual emptiness. His wife, Mildred, sits mesmerized in their "parlor," a room with huge video screens taking up three entire walls. The screens are populated with people who yammer endlessly about absolutely nothing:

No matter when he came in, the walls were always talking to Mildred.

"Something must be done!"

"Yes, something must be *done!*"

"Well, let's not stand and talk!"

"Let's *do* it!"

"I'm so mad I could *spit!*"

What was it all about? Mildred couldn't say. Who was mad at whom? Mildred didn't quite know. What were they going to do? Well, said Mildred, wait around and see.

That may have seemed a little far-fetched 40 years ago, when television was in its infancy, but surely not today, when many people leave the TV on as comforting background noise. I've asked the same kind of questions and gotten similar answers myself.

Mind-Numbing Stimulation

Mildred refers to the inhabitants of the walls as her "family"; to her, they are more real than real life. Remember, this book was written in 1953, when TV had nowhere near the influence and sophistication it has now. Yet Bradbury was able to foresee its mind-emptying potential, its ability, along with other devices, to addict people to sensory stimulation and degrade the capacity to reason—even to feel or enjoy the real world.

Those other devices include "Seashells," radios that fit in both ears. As in today's world, with the ubiquitous Walkman [a personal music player before the iPod] people never have to be without audio stimulation. Mildred wears them in bed all night and when she goes out. And when things get one down, one can go to the amusement park to break windows or crash cars, or drive one's own car at fantastic speeds out into the country to run over wild creatures:

"... Right now I've got an awful feeling I want to smash things and kill things."

"Go take the beetle."

"No, thanks."

"The keys to the beetle are on the night table. I always like to drive fast when I feel that way. You get it up to around ninety-five and you feel wonderful. Sometimes I drive all night and come back and you don't know it. It's fun out in the country. You hit rabbits, sometimes you hit dogs. Go take the beetle."

This casual, remorseless brutality is also applied to fellow humans. Characters in the story occasionally refer to an ongoing wave of murders among teenagers (sound familiar?), and Montag is nearly killed when a carload of joyriding kids tries to run over him for fun. People turn in neighbors for having books, to watch their houses burn. Suicides are also commonplace. Mildred herself takes an overdose of sleeping pills, and Montag calls the stomach-pump squad:

They shut the cases up tight. "We're done." His anger did not touch them. They stood with the cigarette smoke curling around their noses and into their eyes without making them blink or squint. "That's fifty bucks."

"First, why don't you tell me if she'll be all right?"

"Sure, she'll be okay. We got all the mean stuff right in our suitcases here, it can't get at her now. As I said, you take out the old and put in the new and you're okay."

"Neither of you is an M.D. Why didn't they send an M.D. from Emergency?"

"Hell!" The operator's cigarette moved on his lip. "We get these cases nine or ten a night. Got so many, starting a few years ago, we had the special machines built. With the optical lens of course, that was new; the rest is ancient. You don't need an M.D., case like this; all you need is two handymen, clean up the problem in half an hour. Look"—he started for the door—"we gotta go. Just had another call on the old ear thimble. . . ."

The next morning, husband and wife behave as if it never happened.

Memory Loss

While a lesser writer would have to content himself with beating the reader over the head with description and exposition, Bradbury is able to make his nightmare world real with economy and subtlety. The horror never grabs you by the throat as in a Stephen King novel; instead it creeps into your soul almost unnoticed. As in true Polite Totalitarianism, Bradbury's evil lurks behind a bland mask of banal respectability, conformism, and cloying solicitude; most of its subjects never even consciously sense its menace. Warning: don't read this book if you're feeling depressed or paranoid.

Of course, books—nonfiction, novels, poetry, even old magazines—are banned. If you're caught with one, you go to jail or the booby hatch, and your house is burned to the ground. Besides despair and spiritual emptiness, the stupefying combination of frantic sensual gratification and lack of mental exercise also results in the loss of memory. Not only historical memory—everyone has forgotten, for instance, that firemen used to put fires out, not start them—but personal memory as well. Neither Montag or his wife can remember when or where they first met.

Loss of historical memory, of course, is one of the main themes of *1984*. Without it, people are adrift, bereft not only of the cultural signposts and touchstones vital to independent and creative thought but also of any sense of identity or rootedness. However, Montag's world is quite different from that of Winston Smith [from the protagonist in George Orwell's *1984*], and not just because its inhabitants are affluent. Here, the regime hasn't wiped out memory as a means of castrating its subjects. The people have done it to themselves. When Montag begins to have doubts about his job, his superior, Captain Beatty, explains how it happened:

> "Once, books appealed to a few people, here, there, everywhere. They could afford to be different. The world was roomy. But then the world got full of eyes and elbows and

mouths. Double, triple, quadruple population. Films and radios, magazines, books leveled down to a sort of pastepud-
ding norm, do you follow me?"

Beatty goes on to describe how literature was progressively
condensed, boiled down, eviscerated to satisfy people able to
sit still and concentrate for shorter and shorter periods:

> "Speed up the film, Montag, quick. . . . Digest-digests, digest-
> digest-digests. Politics? One column, two sentences, a head-
> line! Then, in mid-air, all vanishes! Whirl man's mind about
> so fast under the pumping hands of publishers, exploiters,
> broadcasters that the centrifuge flings off all unnecessary,
> time-wasting thought!"

Montag Wakes Up

But how did books come to be banned?—

> "Now let's take up the minorities in our civilization, shall
> we? Bigger the population, the more minorities. Don't step
> on the toes of the dog lovers, the cat lovers, doctors, lawyers,
> merchants, chiefs, Mormons, Baptists, Unitarians, second-
> generation Chinese, Swedes, Italians, Germans, Texans,
> Brooklynites, Irishmen, people from Oregon or Mexico. The
> people in this book, this play, this TV serial are not meant
> to represent any actual painters, cartographers, mechanics
> anywhere. The bigger your market, Montag, the less you
> handle controversy, remember that! All the minor minor
> minorities with their navels to be kept clean. . . . Technology,
> mass exploitation, and minority pressure carried the trick,
> thank God. Today, thanks to them, you can stay happy all
> the time, you are allowed to read comics, the good old con-
> fessions, or trade journals."

This is where things get really scary, because to someone
reading the book when it came out, or even 20 years later, the
captain's story must have seemed utterly fanciful. I remember
that when I first read it, it seemed like a convenient scenario-
setting device, taking some latent tendencies in society to ri-

diculous extremes. Today, of course, we know better, what with the increasing propensity to believe in a right not to be offended or disliked, and resulting growth of the list of recognized thought crimes. Idiots wanting to ban [Mark Twain's] *Huckleberry Finn* because it uses the word "nigger" may be hilarious, but they're getting the upper hand.

Montag begins to realize what a wasteland he is living in, and starts to read books filched from his victims, quickly becoming seduced by the rich world that opens up to him. He succumbs to a self-destructive urge and tries to share this new experience with his wife's friends, forcing them to listen to a melancholy poem:

Mrs. Phelps was crying.

The others . . . watched her crying grow very loud as her face squeezed itself out of shape. They sat, not touching her, bewildered with her display. She sobbed uncontrollably. Montag himself was stunned and shaken. . . .

Mrs. Bowles stood up and glared at Montag. "You see, I knew it, that's what I wanted to prove! I knew it would happen. I've always said poetry and tears, poetry and suicide and crying and awful feelings, poetry and sickness; *all* that mush! Now I've had it proved to me! You're nasty, Mr. Montag, you're *nasty!*"

That marks the beginning of the end for Montag, who soon is turned in by his own wife. He winds up on the run from the terrifying "Mechanical Hound," a robot that follows fugitives by their scent and kills with a hypodermic needle. But in an ironic twist, he manages to evade the Hound long enough that the authorities are forced to turn it on an innocent eccentric—eccentric because he is out for a walk—so that the watching TV audience will not get bored and switch channels.

Fahrenheit 451 and Censorship

Censoring a Book on Censorship

Bradbury ends his fable on a note of optimism. Montag is taken in by a group of "walking books" who have each memorized entire volumes, and shortly thereafter, nuclear bombs fall on the city he has just fled. Unfortunately, we can't count on such a salubrious resolution to our own plight.

A final irony is revealed in the new Ballantine edition's afterword, in which Bradbury discusses how his own works, and those of others, have fallen victim to the same tendencies he prophesied. He gets letters suggesting that he "do over" short stories to enhance the roles of women and blacks. Editors of an anthology for students remove a reference to God. He describes a one-volume collection of 400 short stories—*four hundred*—edited for high school kids:

> Every adjective that counted, every verb that moved, every metaphor that weighed more than a mosquito—out! Every simile that would have made a sub-moron's mouth twitch—gone! Any aside that explained the two-bit philosophy of a first-rate writer—lost!

> Every story, slenderized, starved, bluepenciled, leeched and bled white, resembled every other story. Twain read like Poe read like Shakespeare read like Dostoevsky read like—in the finale—Edgar Guest [a prolific and popular early twentieth-century poet whose work most literati considered terrible]. Every word of more than three syllables had been razored. Every image that demanded so much as one instant's attention—shot dead.

One wonders what will happen to Cliffs Notes.

And then, the ultimate irony—censorship of a book about censorship:

> Only six weeks ago, I discovered that, over the years, some cubby-hole editors at Ballantine Books, fearful of contaminating the young, had, bit by bit, censored some 75 separate sections from [*Fahrenheit 451*].

Ask not for whom the bell tolls. It tolls for us.

107

Fahrenheit 451
Teaches That Censorship
Is Counterproductive

Rodney A. Smolla

Rodney A. Smolla, formerly dean of the Washington and Lee University School of Law, is president of Furman University in South Carolina.

In the following selection Smolla reminds readers that Ray Bradbury made it clear that the censorship of Fahrenheit 451's *society was originally initiated by the populace, not the government. The distinction is important, especially when considering how censorship is viewed, legally, in today's society. According to Smolla, any censorship—even that involving the halting of hate speech—is counterproductive and actually makes society less safe and less tolerant.*

Fahrenheit 451, a book heavily about censorship, has experienced an insidious and piecemeal censorship of its own. Over the years the book became particularly popular as assigned reading in schools. This was the good news. The bad news was that over the years, editors at Ballantine Books repeatedly cut little pieces out. The "damns and hells" were particularly ripe for the plucking. In Bradbury's own colorful account, "some cubby-hole editors at Ballantine Books, fearful of contaminating the young, had, bit by bit, censored some 75 separate sections from the novel." Happily, under the enlightened editorship of Judy-Lynn Del Rey, a new Ballantine editor, the book was completely reset and republished, restoring the original text.

Rodney A. Smolla, "The Life of the Mind and a Life of Meaning: Reflections on *Fahrenheit 451*," *Michigan Law Review*, vol. 107, April 2009, pp. 895–912. Copyright © 2009 by Rodney Smolla. Reproduced by permission of the author.

Bradbury would himself turn the novel into a play and an opera, and when he did, he added some additional lines and depth to Fire Chief Beatty, his villain. But while Bradbury was often invited to update his book, expand it, and elaborate on his characters, he never did, perhaps sensing the importance of fidelity to his own original text.

And it is this true text that helps inform our past, our present, and our future. As futurism, *Fahrenheit 451* is fascinating, both for what came true and what did not. Taking stock of the book as futurism, however, is an empty exercise if it is merely assigning prognostication grades. The deeper exercise is to try to determine *why* some things came true and others did not, and what that means, for better or for worse.

Here is a working hypothesis: we have managed to beat back the hounds of censorship, largely through the evolution of enlightened First Amendment doctrines. Yet in a curious irony, in slaying the hounds of censorship we have unleashed and emboldened other hounds. Enlightened free-speech doctrines do not guarantee us enlightened lives. As *Fahrenheit 451* and our present condition both teach, this requires a deeper human effort. To find meaning in life, we must slow down and make time—for the mind, for the senses, and for relationships grounded in genuine connection and respect for our common dignity.

The Anatomy of Censorship

It is all too easy, all too glib, to dismiss censors as tyrants. Yet censors know no political right or political left, no religion, no generation. The censor always believes in the moral righteousness of his or her cause. Indeed, the censor may be—dare we say it?—"right," at least in some sense. History's fair-minded and objective assessment may well be that a particular censor at a particular time and place was motivated to vindicate values widely shared in the society by people of reasonably sound judgment and good will.

Even so, Bradbury's tale is one of inexorable woe to those who censor, even out of altruism. Bradbury seems to be insisting that while it may be possible to incinerate a book, killing the book will not kill its ideas. The life of the mind endures.

Censorship, *Fahrenheit 451* suggests, is often initiated by the populace first and then embraced by the government; it is then that censorship is at its most effective. Censorship is in many respects a natural human instinct, a reflexive impulse. To tolerate the speech we loath is counterintuitive. This is the core of the famous dissenting opinion of Justice [Oliver Wendell] Holmes in *Abrams v. United States* [the 1919 Supreme Court case that made it illegal to urge curtailment of production of materials necessary to the war against Germany with the intent to slow the progress of war]. "Persecution for the expression of opinions seems to me perfectly logical. If you have no doubt of your premises or your power and want a certain result with all your heart you naturally express your wishes in law and sweep away all opposition."

One of the extraordinary features of this extraordinary paragraph is that Holmes is claiming, exactly as the narrative of *Fahrenheit 451* dramatically demonstrates, that persecution for the expression of opinion is *perfectly logical.* When confronted by speech we loath, our natural impulse, individually, socially, and ultimately legally, is to repress it.

It is thus telling that the extreme regime of censorship depicted in *Fahrenheit 451* does not come from the top but from the bottom. The *people* instigate it. The government just goes with the flow. The phrase "political correctness" had not entered our cultural lexicon when *Fahrenheit 451* was written, but that is the sort of phenomenon Bradbury was writing about. At the time Bradbury wrote his novel, First Amendment jurisprudence [the theory and philosophy of the law] could have allowed his dystopian vision to become reality. Fortunately, the Supreme Court has since interpreted the First

Amendment to prohibit such censorship, even when designed to curtail hate speech or to facilitate political correctness.

Censorship of Hate Speech in the Early 1950s

One may see in Beatty's upbeat justifications (in which he claims that it is important not to upset minorities) the premonitions of the American debate over hate speech and the ongoing discourse at American colleges and universities over the propriety and legality of hate-speech codes. The hate-speech illustration is worth exploring in some detail here, for Bradbury makes it clear, both in the novel itself and in his subsequent commentaries about it, that the public desire to quell hate speech is, as he imagines it, one of the most powerful drivers of censorship.

Beatty, justifying the burning of books, says that "we can't have our minorities upset and stirred". What the people want, Beatty argues, is safe speech, not hate speech; they want "pleasure" and "titillation". Books should be burned because they make us think about unpleasant things like racial stereotypes, prejudice, and repression. Beatty makes the point bluntly: "Colored people don't like *Little Black Sambo*. Burn it. White people don't feel good about *Uncle Tom's Cabin*. Burn it". Bradbury reinforces his indictment in his Coda [afterword] to *Fahrenheit 451*:

> The point is obvious. There is more than one way to burn a book. And the world is full of people running about with lit matches. Every minority, be it Baptist / Unitarian, Irish / Italian / Octogenarian / Zen Buddhist, Zionist / Seventh-day Adventist, Women's Lib / Republican, Mattachine / Four Square Gospel feels it has the will, the right, the duty to douse the kerosene, light the fuse. Every dimwit editor who sees himself as the source of all dreary blanc-mange plain porridge unleavened literature, licks his guillotine and eyes the neck of any author who dares to speak above a whisper or write above a nursery rhyme.

Author Ray Bradbury addresses an audience of authors at a convention in 1980. © Roger Ressmeyer/Corbis.

When Bradbury wrote *Fahrenheit 451*, our formal constitutional law doctrines largely encouraged and reinforced the censorship Bradbury describes. He wrote the book in the early 1950s. This was "prehistory" in the timeline of modern First Amendment doctrine. Two decisions, *Chaplinsky v. New Hampshire*, decided in 1942, and *Beauharnais v. Illinois*, decided in 1952, frame the period well.

Real-Life Censorship Cases

Chaplinsky is famous for its succinct expression of the notion that freedom of speech does not include those classes of speech that do little to advance the exposition of ideas and much to injure order and morality:

> There are certain well-defined and narrowly limited classes of speech, the prevention and punishment of which have never been thought to raise any Constitutional problem. These include the lewd and obscene, the profane, the libelous, and the insulting or "fighting" words—those which by

their very utterance inflict injury or tend to incite an immediate breach of the peace. It has been well observed that such utterances are no essential part of any exposition of ideas, and are of such slight social value as a step to truth that any benefit that may be derived from them is clearly outweighed by the social interest in order and morality.

Chaplinsky was followed a decade later by *Beauharnais*, the Supreme Court's first hate-speech decision. In the gap between 1942 and 1952, Adolph Hitler's hate-filled diatribes against Jews had led to mass genocide. It makes perfect historic sense that the Court, with the horrors of the Holocaust fresh in the memory of humankind, would borrow from the theories of *Chaplinsky* to uphold an Illinois law banning hate speech. The Illinois statute in contest made it a crime to portray "depravity, criminality, unchastity, or lack of virtue of a class of citizens, of any race, color, creed or religion" that exposed them "to contempt, derision, or obloquy or which is productive of breach of the peace or riots." The defendant, [Joseph] Beauharnais, was president of a racist Chicago organization, the White Circle League. Beauharnais and his group passed out leaflets calling on Chicago's Mayor and City Council "'to halt the further encroachment, harassment and invasion of white people, their property, neighborhoods and persons, by the Negro.'" The White Circle League's racist diatribe exhorted "'[o]ne million self respecting white people in Chicago to unite,'" proclaiming, "'If persuasion and the need to prevent the white race from becoming mongrelized by the Negro will not unite us, then the aggressions . . . rapes, robberies, knives, guns and marijuana of the negro, surely will.'"

Justice [Felix] Frankfurter wrote the opinion of the Court, which upheld the Illinois law, affirmed the conviction of Beauharnais, and rejected the argument that Beauharnais could not be convicted unless the prosecution proved that his speech posed a clear and present danger of violence. Justice Frankfurter's opinion made an oblique but unmistakable reference to Nazi Germany in his opinion, noting that Illinois did not need to "await the tragic experience of the last three decades" to conclude that laws against racial attacks were necessary to preserve the peace and order of the community. Illinois could thus rightly conclude that purveyors of racial and religious hate "promote strife and tend powerfully to obstruct the manifold adjustments required for free, ordered life in a metropolitan, polyglot community."

Ray Bradbury's novel argues against the thinking of *Beauharnais* and *Chaplinsky*. The complex lesson embedded in *Fahrenheit 451* is that humankind would be better off considering the counterintuitive possibility that a resolve to *not* censor hate speech may actually leave us more safe and secure, more racially tolerant, more bound together as a cohesive moral community.

As Justice Holmes's words suggest, this is a terribly difficult argument to accept at the intuitive level—but history demonstrates its truth. From the Spanish Inquisition to the horrors of the Third Reich, the burning of books was a graphic precursor to mass hysteria, mind control, and paranoia. As Justice [Louis] Brandeis put it, "Men feared witches and burnt women." Yet Brandeis, like Bradbury, pivoted on this observation, arguing that the best way to combat the fear that led men to burn women is to give speech about witches and witch-hunting a free and uncensored venting.

Contemporary
Perspectives
on Censorship

A Contemporary Book Banning Illuminates the Dangers of Censorship

Fenice B. Boyd and Nancy M. Bailey

Fenice B. Boyd is associate professor of learning and instruction at the State University of New York at Buffalo. Nancy M. Bailey is assistant professor of adolescent education at Canisius College in Buffalo.

In the following article Boyd and Bailey caution about the dangers of censorship. To illustrate their argument, they use the example of the 1992 young-adult novel Briar Rose, *by Jane Yolen. Set in Nazi Germany,* Briar Rose *is the story of a young woman nearly dead at the hands of the Nazis, but saved by a gentle gay man who becomes her companion. The subject of intense censoring attempts,* Briar Rose, *say Boyd and Bailey, is poignant in its ability to teach students about important and uncomfortable topics.*

We write this article in early October 2008, coincidentally the same time that the American Library Association (ALA) has, since 1982, designated a Banned Books Week. This is a time, says the ALA, to remind Americans "not to take [a] precious democratic freedom for granted"—the freedom of "unrestricted access to information and ideas regardless of the communication medium used, the content of the work, and the viewpoints of both the author and receiver of information". The ALA's expressed intent for Banned Books Week is to draw attention to First Amendment rights but also to "the power of literature . . . and . . . to the danger that exists when restraints are imposed on the availability of information in a free society".

Fenice B. Boyd and Nancy M. Bailey, "Censorship in Three Metaphors," *Journal of Adolescent & Adult Literacy*, vol. 52, no. 8, 2009. Copyright © 2009 by Cengage Learning Global Rights. Reproduced by permission.

Censorship occurs when published or shared works, like books, films, or art work, are kept from public access by restriction or removal from libraries, museums, or other public venues. Though challenges or outright censorship in our school libraries or classrooms often transpire out of the noblest of reason—most often with the idea of protecting young people from something that someone finds offensive—the ALA sees attempts at censorship, nonetheless, as attempts to restrict someone's "right to read, view, listen to, and disseminate constitutionally protected ideas". We find such censorship of reading or viewing of materials in middle and high school classrooms disturbing and unjust to the rights of both students and teachers.

The Burning of *Briar Rose*

Though book banning was of some interest to us throughout our careers in public school classrooms, our recent investigations related to book banning and censorship started with a seemingly innocuous edition of a fairy tale called *Briar Rose*. In *Briar Rose*, [Jane] Yolen draws upon Grimm's familiar tale of *Sleeping Beauty*, but she recasts the story of the sleeping princess. In Yolen's version, the beautiful princess is a Jew who is not merely asleep, but nearly dead at the hands of the Nazis during the Holocaust. She is saved from death by a group of partisans, all of whom are later killed except one with whom she escapes. Her companion, labeled by the other partisans as the "prince," is a gay man whose gentle friendship and care enable her to live. Yolen's masterfully told tale is by turns horrible and poignant; most important, it is grounded in researched facts and includes descriptions of atrocities and injustices suffered by Jews and homosexuals at the hands of the Nazis at Chelmno, Poland, the site of an extermination camp. It is an important story. The ALA seemed to think so; the organization named *Briar Rose* one of their Best Books for Young

Adults in 1993. The book was also Nebula Award finalist in 1992 and winner of the Mythopoeic Fantasy Award for Adult Literature in 1993.

And yet, there are some who would have the story kept from us. On September 15, 1994, *Briar Rose* was burned on the steps of the Kansas City Board of Education building by the Reverend John Birmingham, a minister of the Power Connection Church, along with members of a group that he represented, the Christian Act Now Coalition. Claiming that *Briar Rose* is a gay-themed book and grouping it with another book about gay men and women and a third book about AIDS, the protesters burned all three books because they saw the topics of homosexuality in the books as dangerous and potentially mind polluting.

Birmingham and his followers used a hibachi [Japanese charcoal grill], to "barbecue" *Briar Rose* and the two other books in Kansas City. What was the point of using the hibachi? we wondered. An easy clean up? Perhaps a subconscious acknowledgment that books really are forms of nourishment? In any case, the ironic juxtaposition of the burning of *Briar Rose* with the book burnings carried out by the Nazis and, especially, with the use of fire to destroy the Jews and homosexuals at camps like Chelmno did not, of course, escape us.

Although parents and guardians have the right to demand that their child will not read a particular book or view a specific film, no one parent or guardian has the right to demand that an entire classroom, school, or district should not read a particular book or view a film. Reading about just such a situation regarding Yolen's book—this time in Chappaqua, N.Y.—we were appalled by the apparent violation of First Amendment rights that might have occurred had the Chappaqua Central School District's Committee Addressing Citizen's Request for Reconsideration of Printed Materials acquiesced to a mother's formal request in November 1994 to have *Briar Rose* withdrawn from all students at Chappaqua's

Bell Middle School where her child was a student. Interestingly, paperwork from the incident revealed that the mother had not read the book, but she was protesting students' access to the book based upon "disturbing passages" on one particular page. Reading about these incidents in Kansas City and Chappaqua led us to investigate other incidences of book challenges and outright censorship and to think deeply about what book censorship means to all of us—educators and students. . . .

Censorship is about restriction and control of intellectual development, and the danger when educators fail to investigate what censorship truly means—for example, by attaching it to metaphors with abundant entailments—is that people will merely "shrug off" the removal of books from libraries and classrooms and fail to see challenges of books as a violation of First Amendment rights. When we strive to explain censorship through metaphor and collect as many entailments as we can to create powerful metaphors, then we can equip educators to truly know the danger of censorship. With this abstract knowledge, educators will be able to move forward with information that may elicit thoughtful responses to challenges that limit teachers' professional decision making and students' paths to a truly democratic society. . . .

Censorship as a Barbed Wire Fence

We believe that reading to make meaning goes far beyond reading for the moment to practice skills; nor is it an exercise for assessment and evaluation purposes. Reading should enable all people, especially young people, to "read the world" as well as the word. This is impossible if censors present obstructions to a clear view of the world—erect "barbed wire"—making it impossible to gain access to the world through vicarious reading experiences. If we think of obstruction as an important entailment of a barbed wire fence, then standing

Members of the Jesus Non-denominational Church in Greenville, Michigan, set fire to numerous items they deemed ungodly, including the Harry Potter novels. AP Images/The Daily News, Lauren Befus.

on the outside looking in is one perception that we use to invoke our metaphor. This perception conveys limited vision and runs both ways. On one side of the fence are the censors and those whom they want to control, standing behind and peeping through the mesh fence and over the barbed wire; on the other side is a book waiting to offer its readers a new, different, and fresh perspective.

Often censors stand on one side of the fence and make uninformed decisions about what books should and should not be read by students. Access to information is denied and more often than not, this denial is due to only a word(s), an isolated concept, or mention of lifestyles that censors find offensive. For instance, *Briar Rose* has been burned due to content related to homosexuality. In fact, *Briar Rose* was "barbecued" because one character was admittedly gay, and we contend that the censors who did that burning stood behind a barbed wire fence blocking students who might read the novel from an opportunity to acquire knowledge. Using blurred and narrowed vision, the book burners denied young people access to information about the inhumane treatment of others and the horrific injustices that innocent people suffered at the hands of the Nazis. How could the censors see and be critical of the gay man in the story and be so completely blind to the savage annihilation of gays during the Holocaust?

The gay character in *Briar Rose* is strong, and because of the censors' misplaced focus, they missed an opportunity to delve more deeply into a historical event that is often omitted from history textbooks written about the Holocaust. This omission perhaps is itself a longstanding form of censorship that blocks school children from a complete view of an important historical event.

Like all great authors, Yolen conducted extensive research about her topic while she was writing her novel. In a letter addressed to Yolen, one of her fans asked, "Is Briar Rose in any way autobiographical? It's too real to be 'made up.' Where did you find out the information about the refugee center at Oswego? Boy have you done a ton of research". Yolen traveled to Poland and spent many months researching the plight of gays during the Holocaust; it is a horrendous and weighty historical event. It is perplexing to think that anyone would destroy the information, ideas, and ideals she offers with the strike of one match.

The Children's Literature Research Collections (CLRC) at the University of Minnesota owns a copy of *Briar Rose*, and on the title page autographed by Yolen, she wrote, "This is the only novel I was ever seriously late in getting in—because it was so damned difficult to write." Here, as she does in other places where she talks about writing about the Holocaust, Yolen implies the physical and emotional strain she experienced while writing *Briar Rose*. In conducting her research about the Holocaust and assigning herself the role of witness, she crossed over the barbed wire and walked through the steel mesh to see clearly the horrific conditions that killed innocent people, including gays. This was, apparently, a deeply moving and laborious task, and it would have been easier to avoid gazing upon the horrors that she saw among the records she examined. Wiping away any narrow, blurred vision, Yolen wrote *Briar Rose* as a clear picture of what the worst of history has left us, and this is a picture that others who fail to cross the barbed wire would deny themselves and others.

Censorship as Patina

A patina is a layer or coating that appears on metals or other surfaces as a result of age or exposure to elements like chemicals or weather. Sometimes, as when it is used to describe wood furniture, the word patina has positive associations, as it indicates a mellow surface that comes with waxing and care, lending "character" to a piece. Other times, however, the word refers to undesirable surfaces caused by corrosion. Nicks, cracks, or crusts cover a more desirable and valuable layer. It is from this latter meaning of the word that we draw our second metaphor.

We see censorship as patina when book challenges and bannings serve to cover, hide, or obscure the ideas that are important for deepening concepts, seeing from different perspectives, and understanding universal qualities of humans and events. Many of us who teach literature do so because of the power of books to stretch and open minds to new ways of looking at the world and to new experiences—albeit vicarious. . . . It is through literature that a child can learn now the world beyond his window works or an adolescent can discover personal attributes that she can weave into who she wants to be. Good literature can also expose human frailty and historical injustice; Willy Loman's story (in *Death of a Salesman* by Arthur Miller, 1949), can be a cautionary tale, as can the one told by Scout Finch (in *To Kill a Mockingbird* by Harper Lee, 1960). [Education scholar K.] Donelson pointed out the great power of books: "Some books challenge us, make us think, make us wonder, make us doubt". It is these books, Donelson says, that make reading so important—but also so dangerous to those who would indoctrinate instead of educate:

> Education implies the right of students to explore ideas and issues without interference from anyone, parent or teacher or administrator. Indoctrination implies the right to force onto students certain values determined by what purports to be the dominant culture. . . . Banning books or screening out "dangerous" issues or "controversial" ideas from classroom discussion typifies a school dedicated to indoctrination. And when the rights to inquire and question and even doubt are denied young people, education inevitably degenerates into indoctrination.

Important Lessons Are Gained from Uncomfortable Topics

When teachers and librarians are forced by challenges from parents or interest groups to remove books from their curricula and library shelves, they must subordinate their pedagogical knowledge about the importance of sharing timeless ideas from good literature to their instincts for self-survival. Thus, these challenges, or the censorship that too often grows out of them, act like a patina, a layer of corrosion that effectively seals beneath itself the wealth of our nation—the values and ideas that we live by in a democratic society.

A challenge to *Briar Rose* in Vermont in 1999 nearly became just such a seal when a mother of a middle school girl asked that Yolen's book be pulled from the school library, thereby removing it—and its important lessons about prejudice, hatred, and injustice—from the reach of all the students in the middle school. Claiming that the book "doesn't have much to say about the Holocaust," the mother said, "The book features widespread profanity and sexual themes. . . ." After a public hearing, a specially formed challenge committee comprised of parents, townspeople, and educators decided to keep the book in the library.

An editorial commenting on the case and its subsequent conclusion in the Barre, Vermont *Times Argus* commended the decision and reminded the newspaper's readers how important ideas about diversity like those presented in *Briar Rose* could be to young people living "in such a homogeneous state" as Vermont. Further addressing the mother's claim that the book made her daughter feel uncomfortable, the editorial continued: "And yet this is the active ingredient in all education: To experience the collision—often violent—between one's own view of the world and the world's view. By postponing that collision, we do our children no favors". The editorial makes clear that hiding the unpleasant or unjust beneath a veneer of denial or distortion of facts does not protect young people, but merely makes them unprepared for what life will present in the future.

The *Times Argus* editorial also reminds readers that tolerance and the ability to respect human differences does not happen automatically: "It must be taught. And if teachers, parents or books don't teach it, then who or what will?". We too wonder about this, especially when we think about the role of book challenges that make teachers want to teach only what is "safe," preventing the possibility of offending parents or any other would-be censors. If books are challenged and disappear from the curriculum, who will teach students to think about and question the status quo when what passes as the norm is privilege for one group at the expense of another, or when denigration of people from diverse backgrounds is so routine that many do not even see it? Books that can open our eyes to white privilege, for example, or to injustices suffered by members of our society are often the very ones that are challenged. "It's no coincidence," said [educator E.] Noll, "that censored literature is usually that which challenges some 'authority' by offering alternative perspectives of reality."

Writing So Others Will Remember

In talks and interviews, Yolen often decries such censorship for violating readers' right to read and also for denying young people a chance to know about their world in ways that will make them better human beings. Speaking to an audience at the International Reading Association's annual conference in 2005 about the mail that she has received from children in regard to *Briar Rose* and the Holocaust, Yolen pointed out the power of books like hers to expand the understanding and awareness of the children who read them. Those who write to her, she said,

> are wrestling—most of them for the first time—with the idea that because they are who they are, born to particular parents, they would have been on one side or the other of a concentration camp's barbed wire. They are struggling to understand how human beings could bring themselves to capture, to torture, to experiment on, to humiliate, to kill other human beings.

Yolen's mail makes quite clear the value of books like *Briar Rose* and what will be lost if we allow such books to be removed from our classrooms and libraries as a result of the challenges of those who would layer their beliefs, like a patina, over the desire of others to know. Such a patina can obscure, cover, even make disappear what is beneath it. It is a fear that important memories will disappear altogether that drives Yolen to write stories like *Briar Rose* though they can be painful to write. . . .

Yet, she tells us, she wrote about the horrors of the concentration camp at Chelmno so that others would remember. Remembering is important for preventing future Holocausts and other atrocities. *Briar Rose* and books like it show us that knowing what the worst of us can do is vital for helping us to strive for what the best of us can be. And yet, those who challenge books like *Briar Rose* would seal those memories away, making them unavailable to young people. We are told often enough the fate of those who fail to learn and remember the lessons of history. Banning books may well be the way to such a fate. Yolen argued, "Censorship—in the classroom, in the library, at the school board level—will make forgetters of us all."

School Censorship of Off-Campus Speech

Julie Hilden

Julie Hilden is a lawyer and a columnist for FindLaw.com.

In the following piece, Hilden questions schools' decisions to punish students for their speech or actions off of school property. In one case cited by Hilden, a middle school student created from her home a false MySpace page for her principal, insinuating that he was a pedophile and a sex addict. The school suspended the student, and later a court confirmed that the suspension was valid since the action was a disruption to the school. Hilden disagrees with this decision, claiming any disruption was minimal and that the principal should have handled the situation better. Most importantly, she says, if schools are going to censor students' speech, the decision should be based on evidence, not speculation.

O n June 3rd, [2010,] . . . the U.S. Court of Appeals for the Third Circuit re-heard two First Amendment cases that involve speech by public-school students. In each case, the speech occurred off campus, but it still resulted in the school's suspending the student involved.

The original panel opinions in the two Pennsylvania-based cases—*Snyder v. Blue Mountain School Dist.*, and *Layshock v. Hermitage School Dist.*—were both issued on February 4th of this year [2010].

The positions of the two sides, upon re-hearing, are quite clear. The ACLU [American Civil Liberties Union], arguing on behalf of the students, contends that speech that occurs out-

Julie Hilden, "Can Public Schools Constitutionally Punish Students' Off-Campus Speech? The U.S. Court of Appeals for the Third Circuit Will Decide," *Find Law Legal News*, June 9, 2010. Copyright © 2010 by FindLaw. Reproduced by permission.

side a public school is also outside the school's jurisdiction: "While children are in school, they are under the custody and tutelage of the school. Once they leave the schoolhouse gate, you've got parents that come into play."

In contrast, the school districts claim that "It's not a matter of where you throw the grenade, it's where the grenade lands." In other words, the districts argue that when students' speech targets the school, it doesn't matter whether the speech itself occurs on-campus or off-campus.

In this column, I'll contrast the facts and holdings of the two Third Circuit panel decisions that were issued on February 4th, and comment on the First Amendment issues they raise.

The *Snyder* Case: The Facts

In the *Snyder* case, a middle-school student—referred to in the court's opinion as "J.S."—and her friend used a home computer to create a fake MySpace profile that included a photo (but not the name) of their school principal.

The profile insinuated that the principal was a sex addict and a pedophile, among other things. But these insinuations could hardly have been taken seriously by anyone who read the page—which was full of slang, poor attempts at humor, and obvious falsehoods. (For instance, the page claimed that the principal lived in Alabama, not Pennsylvania; and it included comments such as this one, purportedly from the principal himself: "i mainly watch-the playboy channel on directv. OH YEAH BITCH!")

J.S. was an honor-roll student who had run afoul of the principal before, but only regarding dress-code violations. She said that she created the profile because she was upset that the principal had yelled at her over one such violation.

After creating the profile, J.S. and her friend subsequently allowed about 22 other students to access it—but because the middle school's computers blocked access to MySpace, it is certain that no student ever viewed the profile while he or she was at school.

After a student known as "B." informed the principal about the MySpace page, J.S. was suspended. The principal asked B. to print out the page and bring the printout to school, which B. did.

The principal then confronted J.S. and her friend and told them that they were suspended, and that he would take legal action against them and their families. He also convinced MySpace to take down the profile. Finally, the principal called the police to look into filing criminal charges based on the profile. However, he dropped the idea after speaking to the police.

In addition to the school suspension, J.S.'s parents punished J.S. for what they said was "a very long time" for posting the profile.

Showing of Disruption Weak at Best

A two-judge majority of the three-judge Third Circuit panel saw no First Amendment violation in J.S.'s suspension. Applying the test set forth by the Supreme Court in *Tinker v. Des Moines Indep. Cmty. Sch. Dist.* [the 1969 Supreme Court case that ruled in favor of students wearing black armbands to protest the Vietnam War, after the students were sent home from school because of the armbands], the panel found that J.S.'s posting could have caused substantial disruption of the school.

(The Supreme Court also decided another student-free-speech case recently, *Morse v. Frederick*, but that case is less relevant than it might seem at first glance: There, the Court allowed a student to be punished for a banner he displayed off school grounds, but the display occurred at a school event, and the Court effectively treated the event as a field trip.)

The panel majority's *Tinker* analysis is weak and unconvincing. The school argued that the actual disruption that occurred consisted of (1) two teachers having to quiet their classes down; (2) a guidance counselor having to proctor an exam so that an administrator could attend a meeting about the profile; and (3) a brief flurry of activity in the hallway because, when the suspension was about to end, students had decorated J.S. and her friend's lockers, and congregated there to welcome them back to school.

(This third supposed disruption, interestingly, seems to have been a First-Amendment-protected protest in its own right—since the students who decorated the lockers apparently did so because they opposed the suspension, so it's not clear that it ought to be included in the analysis. *Tinker's* very point, after all, is that protest is not itself a disruption; instead, there needs to be separate disruption to bring a protest outside the scope of the First Amendment.)

The panel's two-judge majority correctly deemed these three instances of disruption, together, to be too minimal to justify the school's actions. Unfortunately, however, the majority also held that the mere possibility that more disruption might have occurred, had the principal not acted quickly, justified the suspension of J.S.

Moreover, the panel majority treated the MySpace page as if it had been a sober, straightforward claim that the principal was a pedophile. But, as noted above, the page was anything but that. Indeed, the dissenting judge argued that the "profile was so outrageous that no one could have taken it seriously, and no one did," and thus charged that the majority's opinion had turned school boards into censors.

I agree with the dissenting judge—and I would have liked to see some criticism of the principal here, as well. Surely, principals should not be yelling at students who violate dress codes, as J.S. credibly suggested that the principal did, in her case. Setting an example means remaining calm in the face of minor infractions.

And, much more importantly, it is shocking that this principal seriously contemplated filing potentially life-ruining criminal charges against middle-school-age children based entirely on a parodic [spoofing] MySpace posting.

The *Layshock* Case

Like the *Snyder* case, the *Layshock* case involved a middle-school student's suspension based on a fake MySpace profile of a principal that included the principal's photo.

There, too, no one in his or her right mind could have viewed the profile as genuinely having been authored by the principal, or as genuinely making serious allegations against him. And there, too, the student who created the profile also granted a set of school friends access so that they could view it.

Also, in *Layshock*, as in *Snyder*, the principal overreacted by calling the police, but no criminal charges were ultimately filed. And there, too, parents imposed their own sanctions: Justin Layshock was grounded, and was barred by his parents from using his home computer.

However, there are a few factors that were present in *Layshock*, but were not present in *Snyder*: In *Layshock*, the profile spawned more profiles, as other students were inspired to do the same. Also, Justin Layshock accessed the profile in-school, from his Spanish classroom, in order to show it to classmates.

One would think that these factors might mean that Justin's case should have been harder to win than J.S.'s case. Justin's course of conduct included in-school activity, and the additional fake profiles that his profile had spawned could have been deemed disruptive by the court.

But in Justin's case, unlike in J.S.'s, even the school itself agreed—after district-court fact-finding—that, under *Tinker*, no substantial disruption to the school had been caused by Justin's fake MySpace profile.

Moreover, unlike in *Snyder*, the *Layshock* panel focused its scrutiny upon the school, not just the student—pointing out that "Ironically, Justin, who created the least vulgar and offensive profile, and who was the only student to apologize for his behavior, was also the only student punished for the MySpace profiles." Here, the court clearly implied that Justin was being scapegoated—and that it disapproved.

An Available Bright-Line Test

There is a bright-line test available in this context, and schools should adopt it: Off-campus speech shouldn't be the basis for suspension unless it violates civil law (as genuine defamation does), or criminal law (as true threats do).

Alternatively, if the courts do continue to apply *Tinker's* "substantial disruption" test in this context, they ought to make clear that disruption, in this context, doesn't just mean more speech. A fistfight between students in the hallway is one thing; a decorated locker and some gossip is entirely another. And de minimis [minimal] disruptions, such as someone's having to attend a meeting or bring a class to order, should be left out of the equation entirely.

Finally, courts should be wary of finding *Tinker's* test to be fulfilled based on mere speculation as to what would have happened had a principal done nothing. That scenario is unrealistic; if anything, principals are likely to overreact. Moreover, speculation about what could theoretically have happened is out of place and dangerous in the First Amendment context. If speech is going to be censored, it ought at least to be censored based on hard evidence, not wild conjecture.

The Censoring of Students

Amelia McDonell-Parry

Amelia McDonell-Parry is a writer, editor, and blogger in New York City.

In the following essay McDonell-Parry discusses the rights of students to individual speech versus the rights of school districts to prohibit speech that is vulgar or otherwise hurtful to others. In her discussion, she refers to several cases in which students and school districts have disagreed on the issue, including in court. In the end, she says, it must be decided whether something is offensive enough to be censored or whether one should remember that no matter the issue, somewhere, someone will always be offended.

When Megan Reback, a high school senior in Cross River, New York, first read Eve Ensler's *The Vagina Monologues*, she was inspired. Its message about women's empowerment also had a huge impact on her friends Hannah Levinson and Elan Stahl. "It was my idea for us to perform 'My Short Skirt' at our school's open-mike night last March," says seventeen-year-old Megan. "I thought it was really powerful and liberating."

According to the girls, school administrators didn't see it that way. When they found out the piece included the word vagina, the girls were told they would either have to omit that stanza or choose something new to perform. "They didn't feel it would be appropriate for a crowd that could include kids," says Megan. "But the actual audience was high school students and adults. We felt it would defeat the message of *The Vagina Monologues* to alter the piece."

Amelia McDonell-Parry, "The Silent Treatment; What's Okay to Say in School and What Could Get You in Trouble?" *Teen Vogue*, December 2007, pp. 94, 96, 98. Reproduced by permission.

The trio defiantly performed "My Short Skirt" anyway, reading the "offending" sentence in unison: "My short skirt is a liberation flag in the women's army. I declare these streets, any streets, my vagina's country."

For their disobedience, the girls were issued a one-day in-school suspension, which was eventually rescinded when, they say, the school board decided that the girls didn't actually disrupt the educational environment. Ensler showed her support by appearing with them on the *Today* show. "Don't we want our children to resist authority when it's not appropriate and wise?" Ensler said.

Schools Often Err on the Side of Caution

This incident of censorship echoes countless others happening to teens across the country, calling into question when students have the right to free speech and when school administrators have proper authority to silence them.

According to the New York Civil Liberties Union (NYCLU), schools do have the right to prohibit vulgar or lewd speech, but a word like vagina is neither vulgar nor lewd. "Schools should be encouraging students to express themselves freely, not silencing dialogue," Donna Lieberman, executive director of the NYCLU, a division of the American Civil Liberties Union, has said.

But schools often err on the side of caution when presented with anything potentially controversial. Last spring [2007], a group of drama students at Wilton High School in Wilton, Connecticut, compiled the written reflections of U.S. soldiers stationed in Iraq for a play called *Voices in Conflict*. The students were shocked when, they say, their principal, Timothy Canty, canceled all performances.

"We were told that the Iraq War was not a subject that should be discussed in school because there were too many hot buttons," says nineteen-year-old (now-graduated) Wilton student Taylor Telyan. "We were told that we were too young to present a subject of that magnitude, which I found kind of insulting."

Taylor and her fellow classmates also faced harsh criticism from their peers. "This has been big news in our town," eighteen-year-old cast member Erin Clancy explains. "A lot of kids think we're making too big an issue out of it. But this issue is bigger than us; this is about freedom of speech. Plus, the soldiers whose words we were planning to perform are being censored, too."

However, the school's administrators maintained that the fact that the play in its present form could, among other things, offend some students and parents was justification enough for their actions. (Three New York City theaters and one in Connecticut eventually hosted the play this past summer.)

Though both cases of censorship are recent, strict school policies are hardly anything new. Megan, seventeen, from Queens, New York, says boys at her school were not permitted to wear black do-rags because of the possible association with a local gang, and girls aren't allowed to wear revealing clothing—rules she thinks are acceptable. However, "if it came to voicing my opinion," she says, "I would stand up for it. It's important to get every opinion out there, so everything isn't viewed one particular way."

Is Censorship Ever Okay?

What if what you're wearing does voice your opinion? Proving that censorship isn't just a liberal issue, in spring 2006, seventeen-year-old Heidi Zamecnik of Naperville, Illinois, wore a T-shirt that declared, be happy, not gay the day after the National Day of Silence, which protests harassment of gay and transgender students in schools.

According to Zamecnik's suit, she wanted to wear the shirt to school to express her "conviction that true happiness can-

Student Makenzie Hatfield used her free-speech rights to fight against her school's ban of Pat Conroy books. Similar incidents of censorship are being echoed in schools across the country. AP Images/Jeff Gentner.

not be found through homosexual behavior." One school administrator asked her to remove the shirt, while another told her to cross out "not gay" with a marker. Zamecnik filed a suit against the school, saying they violated her First Amendment rights. [A federal judge ruled in favor of the school and its right to dictate a dress code.]

Interestingly, the Supreme Court's ruling on free speech in schools, in 1969, also involved a garment. When students wore black armbands to school to protest the Vietnam War, they too were punished, but the Supreme Court eventually decided students do not "shed their constitutional rights to freedom of speech or expression at the schoolhouse gate." So shouldn't Zamecnik be regarded by that standard?

"I think there are times when censorship is okay, like when someone is making fun of someone else," says Spencer, nineteen, from Victoria, Texas. "[Zamecnik] is trying to strip someone of their right to sexuality." "Even though she is allowed to express her opinion," says Megan, "it's not right to do it at someone else's expense. That shirt could have hurt a lot of people."

In 2002, Joseph Frederick, then a student at a Juneau, Alaska, high school, displayed a banner that read bong hits 4 jesus on a public sidewalk outside of his school. Principal Deborah Morse suspended him for the offense, which she called promoting illegal drug use and which Frederick called "a joke." Frederick took the fight to court—all the way up to the Supreme Court, in fact.

In June 2007, the Supreme Court ruled in favor of Morse and the Juneau school district, thereby demonstrating where the highest law of the land currently stands on free speech in the educational domain.

Regardless of where you and your school's administrators think the line should be drawn, there is a common thread through all four cases—fear of openly discussing tough issues that might be offensive to people. But as Megan Reback says,

"Someone, somewhere, is always going to be offended by something. You have to talk about the things that are controversial in order to learn anything."

Censorship Is Sometimes Necessary

Amelia Jimenez

When she wrote this article, Amelia Jimenez was a junior at Hershey High School in Pennsylvania and a Patriot-News *Davenport fellow.*

In this article, high school student Jimenez reminds student writers that, when writing for school newspapers, they must expect to be censored sometimes. Jimenez identifies two reasons that students should be censored: first, inflammatory remarks could offend and harm others; also, having such statements censored prepares students for living in a politically correct world. At the same time, Jimenez believes school administrators should censor only when necessary, especially since the First Amendment protects freedom of speech. With mutual respect between students and administrators, a balance can be struck.

"Give me the liberty to know, to utter and to argue freely according to conscience, above all liberties," once said [English poet] John Milton.

Thanks to the First Amendment, everyone has the right to freely express his or her ideas. Still, as Milton said, these expressions must be ethically made.

While writing for [Pennsylvania's] Hershey High School's newspaper, *The Broadcaster,* I have learned about the importance of and gained a new appreciation for journalism ethics. Because high school journalists are still learning ethics, rational censoring is imperative in school newspapers.

School administrators should not abuse their right to censor. In the same way, students should not abuse their right to express themselves.

Amelia Jimenez, "High School Censorship: Striking a Balance," *Patriot-News: PennLive .com,* April 19, 2009. Copyright © 2009 by The Patriot-News. All rights reserved. Reprinted and/or used with permission.

Professional newspapers do not publish inappropriate or offensive content even though they have complete freedom of the press. For example, *The Patriot-News* discards many improper cartoons. Publishing such items would diminish the professional and ethical image of the staff as well as upset readers of the newspaper.

Limiting what appears in school newspapers teaches students that it is inappropriate to publish certain material and that, if the students ever work for a professional newspaper, editors might censor their work.

In a report about the Hazelwood vs. Kuhlmeier Supreme Court case of 1988 [which maintained that public school newspapers are subject to a lower level First Amendment protection than other newspaper], the Fund for Free Expression stated, "[Students] are learning in practice what it is like to endure censorship and restrictions of free expression." In essence, censoring prepares students for a politically correct world.

Aside from contributing to lessons, censoring also protects students' rights. The *Tinker vs. Des Moines* Supreme Court case of 1969 ruled that school officials may censor when it is "necessary to avoid material and substantial interference with school work or discipline or the rights of others."

The Newseum's Learning Center class "You Can't Say That in School?!" teaches that having no limits in schools takes away the ability to learn. "There must be a balance between learning and expressing," says the class' instructor Kirsti Potter.

A school's main function is to provide an academic education. The *Hazelwood vs. Kuhlmeier* case determined that school administrators may eliminate content that is inconsistent with the school's educational mission.

Censoring school newspapers not only strengthens educational programs but also protects students and schools. If students publish offensive, defamatory, problematic content, those affected or insulted are likely to sue those responsible for the publication. By stopping unethical material from hitting the stands, schools are preventing greater conflicts.

As decided in the *Hazelwood vs. Kuhlmeier* case, school officials also might remove topics that are potentially sensitive. Although high school students are already exposed to mature issues, many parents do not approve of schools providing information on topics such as sex, weapons or drugs. Schools must make sure that the publication of such material is carefully monitored in order to avoid parental concerns.

Yet, it is important to remember that all newspapers are ways of communication. Young people need to express their ideas so that they can grow to be opinionated adults.

They have the right to convey their viewpoints, as long as those viewpoints do not interfere with the rights of others.

Therefore, the subject matter in school newspapers should not be limited. Instead, students must write fairly, ethically and accurately. For example, Hershey High School's newspaper recently tackled our school's dance policy; the staff used reliable sources and quotes.

Thomas Paine once said, "When we speak of right we ought always to unite with it the idea of duties: rights become duties by reciprocity."

Student journalists have the right to report, but they also have the duty to use ethics when doing so. School administrations have the right to control the student body, but they also have the duty to foster a supporting community that encourages students to speak their minds.

If students publish consciously and administrations censor consciously, there is a balance between school and student rights.

Governments Should Not Try to Censor the Internet

Fons Tuinstra

Fons Tuinstra is director of the China Speakers Bureau.

In the following article Tuinstra discusses the ongoing tension between the force of the Internet and the power of authoritarian national governments. As a result of this clash, numerous national leaders have tried to limit, or even shut down, the Internet in their countries. In the end, argues Tuinstra, it is nearly impossible to deny society access to the Internet because people will continually find ways to get around the barriers put before them.

The political situations and protests in Tehran, Iran and Xinjiang, China unfolded as this summer [of 2009] began. So, too, did the latest round in the inevitable clash of the Internet's borderless communications and governments' attempt to rein them in. Similar tensions from earlier confrontations offer glimpses of the complicated relationship between the power of the Web and the question of how authoritarian rulers exert their power in return.

Follow reports on Internet censorship, and the road leads not only to China, Kenya and Iran, where governments have attempted to clamp down on the use of social media, but to Australia, Germany and the United States, where companies develop software to enable such censorship. In such stories resides the illusion that the Internet actually can and will be controlled. This myth of control is perpetuated by many in

Fons Tuinstra, "Internet Censorship: The Myth, Off Told, and the Reality: Protests in Iran and China Have Spotlighted the Use of Social Media, Showing Its Power in Finding Ways to Push Information Past Barriers Set Up by Government," *Nieman Reports*, vol. 63, no. 3, 2009. Copyright © 2009 by The Nieman Foundation. Reproduced by permission.

the old media, some of whom must be hoping, as they tell these stories, that their top-down approach to news gathering and distribution still has a chance against the tsunami of people-generated information that has devastated so many legacy media brands and likely will destroy more in the years ahead. (Of course, there is also the argument that when freedom of information and press is at stake, siding with those who urge restraint seems odd. But let's not make things too complicated.)

In the telling of this Internet censorship story, a psychological component is almost certainly in play. This is, after all, a time when journalists feel their livelihood is under siege from the Internet. Although some at legacy news organizations have embraced parts of the Internet, a foreboding fear of its power and consequences prevails. Stories about the success of Internet censorship, illusionary as they might be, can provide relief to those who feel embattled and who hope that in some way the Internet can be controlled, in part because their survival depends on it.

Attempts to Control the Internet Fall Short

Such hope is misguided. Add to this a trail of inaccurate reporting about what's been happening in Xinjiang—and last year in Tibet—and a crisis of mistrust has been created. The increasingly active online community knows the Chinese news media cannot be trusted given their government control. But Western media, too, are systematically scrutinized for what is regarded as their biased reporting. In China, at least, I have observed that the Western press have lost the high ground of reliability they used to hold. Drastic cuts in funding for foreign correspondents have had an impact on the quality and diversity of reporting. Now, this force of online scrutiny cannot be stopped. Attempts to block it are answered with new, inventive ways around whatever barriers are constructed.

China is known for its strict Internet censorship, which has included blocking sites such as Google and Twitter. AP Images/Ng Han Guan.

Technically, a government can shut down the Internet. But there are reasons—economic and political—that trump censorship and help to explain why it seldom does. China could have closed the entire Internet in Xinjiang province in July after riots there resulted in nearly 200 deaths and more than 1,000 wounded. In fact, reports from the region indicated that the Internet was not accessible for some time. Because Xinjiang is a marginal part of China, the consequences of temporarily bringing its economy to a standstill are not huge for the country as a whole. However, when China and Iran, as nations, experience political crisis and citizen protest, they cannot afford to close down the digital highway of information given the impact this would have on commerce and the economy. North Korea is the only country that has fully controlled the Internet, though few countries seem to be willing to follow its example.

Throughout the rest of China, the response of the telecommunication operators was more moderate during the Xinjiang crisis. Twitter, YouTube, some local clones of Twitter, and a few other sites were shut down for a time. I watched as the number of tweets from China was reduced a bit, but after three hours they were up to speed again. Although the information flow was more limited—and most of the Western and Chinese media mostly stuck to rise same story lines they'd been reporting since the start of the riots—a flood of fresh video clips, digital commentaries, and blog posts made it around the government's Internet barriers.

This situation was described in the *China Digital Times* in early July:

> Nevertheless, many Chinese netizens [a person who uses the Internet] are still managing to access outside information and publish their views on the situation. For example, photographs taken by foreign journalists are being spread online; people are finding ways to post on Twitter despite the site being blocked; and netizens are still finding ways to post their views to BBS [bulletin boards] forums. Overseas Chinese Web sites and communities are also playing a role by posting information and discussions, many of which can find their way back into Chinese cyberspace.

With the Internet, Conversation Rules

Stories from Xinjiang, some true, some not, kept arriving in my computer. Some Internet users shared information about ways to work around the Internet blocks, helpful to those who had not yet discovered such tools. This was testimony to the ineffectiveness of what some in the Western media were describing as an Internet "crackdown." In the meantime, Chinese officials, with years of experience in filtering the Internet, were practicing well the lessons they've learned: Use their force sparingly since this prevents a new generation of Internet users from discovering the numerous ways netizens have figured out to thwart their efforts.

Every now and then, however, one of China's senior leaders panics and suddenly the country finds not only Twitter, but even Google has been blocked. Earlier this year, this happened for a short while. Such measures prove to be not only ineffective in terms of stopping the flow of information, but the economic effects of such a closure, if it was to last for some time, would be massive. Because of this, even these impulses to undertake larger scale Internet blockages disappear after a short while. Additionally, the Chinese have learned, too, how to use the Internet as their watchful eyes and ears. At times, the government's public relations officials improve even their spin as a result of using the Internet as a vehicle for disseminating information. Shutting down or restraining the Internet, especially in times of crises, would make it impossible for those eyes and ears to pick up information about what's happening, and it would shut down the government's channels for countering with their own messages.

In these ways, the Internet presents a very different medium from radio, TV and print in terms of how governments respond in times of severe crisis. Whereas a government takeover of broadcast stations or print publications is a fairly straightforward operation, this isn't so with the Internet. As the Internet is teaching, conversation rules. Those who want to share information will employ whatever digital tool can be used to keep the flow of information going. Platforms still matter, but they can be replaced if they are shut down. And shutting them down isn't as simple as it used to be.

For Further Discussion

1. In Chapter 1 Ray Bradbury reveals a very imaginative version of the ideal city in his interview with John Geirland, while Sam Weller describes Bradbury's beautiful green hometown and colorful ancestry. How do you think Bradbury's upbringing and family ancestry influenced his vast imagination and ability to write? If he grew up in different circumstances, do you think he would have become the writer he is? Why or why not? How does Bradbury's "ideal city" compare and contrast with the city he created in *Fahrenheit 451*?

2. In Chapter 2 Edward E. Eller quotes Ray Bradbury as saying ". . . when Hitler burned a book I felt it as keenly, please forgive me, as his killing a human, for in the long sum of history they are one and the same flesh." How do you think the book people in *Fahrenheit 451* would respond to this quotation? Do you think Bradbury's creation of the character of Mildred Montag symbolized his belief that if you killed books you killed humans? Why or why not?

3. In Chapter 2 it is widely noted that *Fahrenheit 451*'s environment of extreme censorship was initiated by the populace, not the government. As Erika Gottlieb puts it: "Bradbury does not represent the burning of books and the persecution of writers and readers as an *effect* of political dictatorship; rather, he created a society that became a dictatorship *as a result of* burning books." What similar comments do Rodney A. Smolla and David Seed offer? What are the significant differences between censorship

initiated by the public versus the government? Do you think one would have more lasting consequences over the other? Why or why not?

4. In Chapter 3 Amelia McDonell-Parry quotes two high school students with contrasting views on censorship. According to one student, "I think there are times when censorship is okay, like when someone is making fun of someone else." In contrast, another student claims, "Someone, somewhere, is always going to be offended by something. You have to talk about the things that are controversial in order to learn anything." Do you agree with either statement, or can you offer a different perspective on the issue? What are your reasons for holding the opinion you have?

For Further Reading

Margaret Atwood, *The Handmaid's Tale*. Toronto: McClelland and Stewart, 1985.

Ray Bradbury, *Dandelion Wine*. Garden City, NY: Doubleday, 1957.

———, *Dark Carnival*. Sauk City, WI: Arkham House, 1947.

———, *Green Shadows, White Whale*. New York: Knopf, 1992.

———, *The Halloween Tree*. New York: Knopf, 1972.

———, *I Sing the Body Electric!* New York: Random House, 1969.

———, *The Illustrated Man*. Garden City, NY: Doubleday, 1951.

———, *The Machineries of Joy*. New York: Simon and Schuster, 1964.

———, *The Martian Chronicles*. Garden City, NY: Doubleday, 1950.

———, *Something Wicked This Way Comes*. New York: Knopf, 1962.

Anthony Burgess, *A Clockwork Orange*. London: Penguin, 1962.

Aldous Huxley, *Brave New World*. London: Chatto and Windus, 1932.

George Orwell, *Nineteen Eighty-Four*. Middlesex, UK: Penguin, 1949.

Ayn Rand, *Anthem*. London: Cassell, 1938.

Bibliography

Books

John Bankston	*Ray Bradbury*. New York: Chelsea House, 2011.
Gene Beley	*Ray Bradbury: Uncensored! The Authorized Biography*. Lincoln, NE: iUniverse, 2006.
Cathy Byrd and Susan Richmond	*Potentially Harmful: The Art of Censorship*. Atlanta: Georgia State University, 2006.
Joan DelFattore	*What Johnny Shouldn't Read: Textbook Censorship in America*. New Haven, CT: Yale University Press, 1992.
John Eller	*Ray Bradbury: The Life of Fiction*. Kent, OH: Kent State University Press, 2004.
Matthew Fishburn	*Burning Books*. New York: Palgrave Macmillan, 2008.
Nat Hentoff	*Free Speech for Me—but Not for Thee: How the American Left and Right Relentlessly Censor Each Other*. New York: HarperCollins, 1992.
Rebecca Knuth	*Burning Books and Leveling Libraries: Extreme Violence and Cultural Destruction*. Westport, CT: Praeger, 2006.

Paul Krassner   *In Praise of Indecency: The Leading*
                     Investigative Satirist Sounds Off on
                     Hypocrisy, Censorship and Free
                     Expression. San Francisco: Cleis Press,
                     2009.

Diane Ravitch   *The Language Police: How Pressure*
                     Groups Restrict What Students Learn.
                     New York: Knopf, 2003.

Sam Weller   *The Bradbury Chronicles: The Life of*
                     Ray Bradbury. New York: William
                     Morrow, 2011.

Sam Weller   *Listen to the Echoes: The Ray*
                     Bradbury Interviews. Brooklyn, NY:
                     Melville House, 2011.

Periodicals

Carl Abbott   "The Light on the Horizon:
                     Imagining the Death of American
                     Cities," *Journal of Urban History*,
                     January 2006.

Constance   "Sensitivity or Censorship?" *Science*,
Holden   February 25, 2005.

Erin Downey   "Just Open the Door: Banned Books
Howerton   (and a Librarian!) in the Classroom,"
                     Young Adult Library Services, Spring
                     2007.

Joseph Janes   "Censorship Gets Smart," *American*
                     Libraries, November 2009.

Dave Jenkinson   "Selection & Censorship: It's Simple
                     Arithmetic," *School Libraries in
                     Canada*, vol. 21, no. 4, 2002.

Jamie Kelly   "Missoula School Publications Policy
                     Debated by Panel, Students,
                     Superintendent," *Missoula (MT)
                     Missoulian*, July 29, 2010.

Frank D.   "Student Journalism Confronts a
LoMonte   New Generation of Legal Challenges,"
                     *Human Rights: Journal of the Section
                     of Individual Rights & Responsibilities*,
                     Summer 2008.

David L.   "School Censorship: It Comes in a
Martinson   Variety of Forms, Not All Overt,"
                     Clearing House, May/June 2008.

Credence   "The Folly of Politically Correct
McFadzean   Censorship," *Leader-Post* (Regina,
                     Saskatchewan), September 8, 2009.

Rafeeq O.   "Bradbury's *Fahrenheit 451*,"
McGivern   *Explicator*, Spring 1996.

Kent Oliver   "Libraries Must Protect the Freedom
                     to Read," *Forbes*, July 8, 2010.

Shirrel Rhoades   "One-on-One with the Author: Ray
                     Bradbury," *Saturday Evening Post*,
                     September/October 2009.

Gary Scharrer   "Poll: Public School Curriculum
                     Should Be Left to Educators," *Dallas
                     Morning News*, Austin Bureau, July
                     13, 2010.

Jennifer
Steinhauer

"At 88, a Writer Fights for Libraries, and Tells a Few of Life's Tales," *New York Times*, June 20, 2009.

Roger Sutton

"Here's Why It's Censorship," *Horn Book Magazine*, May/June 2007.

Cynthia Weber

"'Fahrenheit 9/11': The Temperature Where Morality Burns," *Journal of American Studies*, April 2006.

Sam Weller

"The Art of Fiction No. 203: Interview with R. Bradbury," *Paris Review*, Spring 2010.

David Wright

"Brother Ray," *Alki*, July 2009.

Index